THRIVE NOW!

EIGHT PROVEN KEYS TO
UNLOCK THE LIFE YOU WANT

Thrive Now!

Copyright © 2025 by Paul Endress. All rights reserved.

No part of this book may be used or reproduced in any manner whatsoever without written permission except in the case of brief quotations embedded in critical articles or reviews.

The content of this book does not constitute the establishment of a therapeutic relationship between you and the author. This content is for educational and entertainment purposes only, and is not a substitute for financial, medical, or psychological consultation, treatment or advice.

If you have any medical or psychological condition or distressing psychological or medical symptoms, consult a physician before doing anything suggested in this book.

For information contact:
Cardinal House Press
4800 Linglestown Rd.
Suite 302
Harrisburg, PA 17112

www.thrive365.net

FIRST EDITION

ISBN: 979-8-9855786-3-8

LEAVE THE ROCKS BEHIND!

LIGHTEN THE LOAD AND MOVE FORWARD

Picture this: You're hiking up a scenic mountain trail. The sun warms your skin, the crisp air fills your lungs, and every step brings you closer to the breathtaking summit.

You're eager, energized, and ready for the challenge ahead.

But as the trail winds upward, something feels off. Your backpack seems heavier with each step.

At first, you brush it off—maybe you're just tired.

But eventually, the weight is too much to ignore so you stop, unbuckle the straps, and take a look inside.

Rocks.

Some small, some large, but all of them weighing you down.

Leave the Rocks Behind!

The surprising thing is that you don't remember putting them there. You're not even sure how long they've been in your pack.

But one thing is clear: carrying them has been making your journey harder than it needs to be.

Life works the same way.

We set out with excitement, chasing dreams, building careers, and strengthening relationships, only to find ourselves struggling under invisible weight—old habits, limiting beliefs, or patterns of thinking we didn't even realize were holding us back.

And the frustrating part?

No one ever taught us to stop and check our pack.

That's where *Thrive Now!* comes in.

Unlike other books that tell you to "just work harder" or "think positive," I've written *Thrive Now!* to help you identify what's actually holding you back—and shows you how to **remove those hidden obstacles for good.**

Success isn't just about adding more—more skills, more strategies, more effort. Sometimes, **the fastest way to thrive is to lighten the load.**

That's exactly why I've written *Thrive Now!* to show you how to recognize the hidden obstacles slowing you down and remove them, one by one.

If you're ready to **stop struggling under unnecessary weight** and start moving forward with clarity and confidence, you're in the right place.

Thrive Now! is your guide to uncovering and releasing the mental roadblocks that stand between you and the life you've always imagined.

With small but powerful shifts, you'll clear the path to more success, fulfillment, and momentum—starting now.

Let's start by asking an important question:

WHAT IS SUCCESS, REALLY?

For a long time, I thought success had a clear finish line—a moment where I'd finally *arrive.*

Maybe it was hitting a certain income level, landing the right opportunity, or achieving a goal that looked impressive from the outside.

But over the years, I've learned that **success isn't a destination—it's a direction.**

It's not a job title, a bank balance, or a highlight reel that looks great on social media.

Success is personal.

It's about moving consistently toward what truly matters to you—building a life that reflects your values, dreams, and goals.

I'll never forget a conversation I had with a friend years ago.

He had just sold his company for a life-changing amount of money, something he had worked for over a decade to achieve.

By every traditional measure, he was "successful." But when I asked him how he felt, he sighed and said, *"Honestly? A little lost."*

That moment stuck with me.

It made me realize that **success isn't about reaching one big milestone—it's about what you're building every single day.**

If your achievements don't align with what truly matters to you, they won't feel fulfilling. And if you're constantly waiting for "someday" to feel successful, you'll never allow yourself to enjoy the journey.

That's why I wrote *Thrive Now!*—because success isn't about checking boxes or meeting other people's expectations.

It's about creating a life that feels right to you. And the best part?

You don't have to wait to thrive—you can start right now.

RETHINKING FAILURE: IT'S NOT FALLING—IT'S STOPPING

If success isn't about reaching a finish line, then what about failure?

For a long time, I thought failure meant falling short, missing the mark, or facing setbacks. It's easy to believe that if something doesn't work out the way you planned, you've failed.

But over the years, I've realized that real **failure isn't about stumbling—it's about stopping.**

Years ago, I worked with a business owner who had poured his heart and all of his resources into launching a new product, but after months of effort, it wasn't gaining traction.

Frustrated, he told me, *"Maybe this just isn't meant to be."*

He was ready to walk away, convinced he had failed.

But instead of quitting, I encouraged him to take a step back and ask, *"What's not working, and what can I adjust?"*

Asking a great question like this (page 89) gave him ideas he hadn't previously thought of and he didn't give up.

He refined his approach, tweaked his messaging, and reconnected with his purpose. A few months later, his product finally got traction and started to take off.

The difference?

He didn't let obstacles define his story—he used them to recalibrate and move forward.

That's the truth: You are always one decision away from progress. And that's why every chapter of Thrive Now! ends with specific steps you can take immediately.

Every challenge is an opportunity to adapt, grow, and keep going. **Failure only happens when you let frustration or doubt convince you to quit.**

Success isn't about endlessly stacking up achievements, possessions, or credentials.

It's a journey and this is <u>your</u> journey, and every step forward is worth celebrating.

So, if you stumble, don't stop.

Adjust, learn, and keep going—because your next breakthrough could be just one step away.

YOUR JOURNEY, YOUR PACE

The best part about *Thrive Now!*?

It's not a one-size-fits-all formula.

Your path to success is unique, and so are the steps you need to take.

Wherever you are right now, *Thrive Now!* meets you there.

You don't have to read it cover to cover in one sitting (though you're welcome to!). Instead, think of it as a toolkit—a set of powerful keys designed to unlock your potential.

Before you start, take a moment to reflect: What's one area of your life where you feel stuck or weighed down?

Keep that in mind as you move through the book—because that's where your transformation begins.

Pick the keys that resonate with you **right now** and dive in. The rest will be here when you're ready.

READY TO THRIVE? LET'S GO.

Every great transformation starts with a single step.

So, let's lighten the load, remove the roadblocks, and unlock the success waiting for you.

It's time to Thrive Now!

THE KEY SHIFT™

Small shifts. Major breakthroughs.

HOW TO REMOVE THE ROCKS AND THRIVE NOW

There's something freeing about realizing that success isn't just about adding more—it's about removing what's slowing you down.

Sure, you will probably need to make some decisions, build new skills, or take on fresh challenges along the way. But before any of that, **the first and most important step is clearing the roadblocks** that have been keeping you stuck.

I remember talking to Camila, a talented professional who felt completely stuck in her career. She kept signing up for new courses, reading leadership books, and networking—but nothing seemed to change.

When we dug deeper, she realized it wasn't a lack of skills that was holding her back. It wasn't a lack of effort that was holding her back—it was staying busy instead of making meaningful progress.

She filled her days with tasks, attended every meeting, and worked late, thinking that sheer effort would lead to success. But deep down, she wasn't focusing on what truly mattered.

Once she recognized that productivity isn't about doing more but about doing what moves you forward, everything shifted.

She didn't need to add more to her plate—she needed to focus her energy on what would create real results. She began prioritizing high-impact tasks, setting clear goals, and finishing what she started.

Within months, her work started getting noticed, and she landed the leadership role she had been striving for—**not because she worked harder, but because she worked smarter.**

That's why these eight keys matter so much.

They're not about adding more to your life—they're about letting go of what's been weighing you down.

By removing the hidden obstacles—whether it's short-term thinking, hesitation, distractions, the wrong questions, or self-doubt—you create a clear path for success to happen faster and with less struggle.

When you stop carrying unnecessary weight, you free yourself to move forward with confidence, focus, and momentum.

Yes, you'll still need to make decisions and develop new skills along the way. But when you stop carrying unnecessary weight, everything becomes easier. And once you start moving freely toward what you want, there's no limit to what you can achieve.

THE THREE STEPS OF THE KEY SHIFT™ PROCESS

Step 1: Recognize the hidden obstacles

Success doesn't just come from effort—it comes from identifying what's been slowing you down.

Maybe it's an old belief that no longer serves you. A habit that keeps pulling you back. A pattern of thinking you never questioned.

Once you see it, you can use the framework at the end of each key to finally **let it go.**

Step 2: Change your mindset

At the end of each chapter, you'll find powerful **Key Shift questions** designed to rewire your thinking and behavior in small but **transformational** ways. These shifts create momentum—fast.

Step 3: Take immediate action

The fastest way to change your life isn't through years of trial and error. **It's by making small shifts now** and that's exactly why we start with the *Master Key* on page 15.

Move Forward One Key at a Time

Each of the eight keys unlocks a different part of your personal and professional growth, helping you move from where you are now to where you *know* you're meant to be.

Maybe you feel stuck.

Maybe you're already moving but know there's *more* waiting for you. Either way, these keys will give you the clarity, confidence, and momentum to move forward—starting today.

Best of all?

You don't have to wait.

The moment you start using just *one* of these keys, you'll feel the shift.

The thriving life you've been looking for is closer than you think.

Are you ready to unlock it?

Where to Start

THE EIGHT KEYS

WHERE TO START

Now it's time to unlock the eight keys that power the *Thrive Now! Key Shift™*—a framework designed to remove obstacles and open the door to your full potential.

Each key tackles a specific challenge— one of the hidden "rocks" in your backpack that have been quietly weighing you down.

These obstacles may have been making progress harder than it needs to be, without you even realizing it. But once you remove them, everything changes.

Each key focuses on a different area of life, providing a shift in thinking and action that helps you move forward—faster, with less effort, and with more clarity.

But **where should you start?**

That depends on where you are right now and what's been holding you back.

Use this quick guide to decide which key to start with:

THE MASTER KEY
GET STARTED. KEEP GOING
Use This Key to Get Unstuck and Start Moving

If you've ever felt stuck—not because you're lazy, but because you don't know where to start, feel overwhelmed by too many choices, or are afraid of making the wrong move—this key helps you break through the fog and start moving toward the life you want.

The Master Key shows you how real progress begins: with a small step, followed by consistent action

- ☑ What have you been thinking about doing for a while— but still haven't started?

- ☑ Are you waiting for the "perfect time" or more information before you act?

- ☑ Have you lost trust in yourself, or feel unmotivated?

The Master Key gives you the simple pattern that **breaks the cycle of stuckness**:

Start small. Build momentum. Stay consistent. That's how you unlock the life you want.

This Master Key starts on page 15.

Where to Start

KEY #1
FUTURE-PROOF YOUR DECISIONS
Make choices today that create better results tomorrow.

If your decisions sometimes lead to problems down the road or making life harder than it needs to be—this key will help you see beyond the immediate choice.

- Has a past decision ever led to unexpected problems that you wish you had seen coming?"
- Are you dealing with the same challenges over and over?
- Have you ever changed jobs, goals, or relationships and been surprised about how it affected your future?

With this key you'll learn how to make decisions that not only work for today but also create better results down the road.

This key starts on page 47.

KEY #2
WORK SMART TO FINISH STRONG
It's not about doing more.
It's about doing what truly matters.

It's easy to stay busy, but real progress comes from doing the right things, not just more things.

- At the end of the day, do you feel exhausted but unsure of what you actually accomplished?

- Are you great at starting things but struggle to see them through to the finish?

- Is your to-do list always full, but you're not getting closer to your real goals?

This key helps you cut through the distractions, direct your energy toward meaningful outcomes, and follow through so **your hard work creates real impact.**

Work Smart To Finish Strong starts on page 69.

Where to Start

KEY #3
ASK BETTER QUESTIONS AND THRIVE FASTER
Unlock new possibilities by asking better questions

If you're not getting the results you want, the problem might not be your actions—it might be the questions you're asking.

- Do you find yourself second-guessing decisions after it's too late to change them?

- When trying to solve a problem, do you often feel stuck, unsure of where to start?

- Do you sometimes feel like your choices are limited, even when you know there must be a better way?

This key shows you how to break free from limiting thinking, **uncover hidden opportunities**, and find better solutions by asking smarter, more purposeful questions that reveal hidden obstacles, solve problems, gain clarity, and open the door to new possibilities that move you forward—faster.

Start on page 89.

KEY #4
FIND THE SWEET SPOT BETWEEN PASSION, STRENGTHS & NECESSITY

Balance what you love, what you're good at, and what you need to do.

The advice to *"follow your passion and do what you love"* is exciting—it fuels dreams, ignites motivation, and makes success feel limitless.

But sometimes **passion alone isn't enough.**

True fulfillment happens when you align your passion with your natural strengths and apply both in a way that works in the real world.

- Have you ever pursued something you were passionate about—only to realize it was preventing you from getting something else important?

- Do you feel torn between what excites you and what you're naturally great at?

- Are you struggling to turn your passion into something sustainable and impactful?

Passion can light the fire, but your natural strengths are the fuel that keeps it burning. When you build on your strengths, **progress feels easier, confidence grows, and success becomes more natural.**

You'll find this key on page 107.

Where to Start

KEY #5
SEE CLEARLY, DREAM BOLDLY
Combine ambition with a clear understanding of reality.

It's exciting to dream big, but ignoring reality can leave you stuck and frustrated.

- Do you ever get excited about a big idea but struggle with the practical steps necessary for success?

- Is there a hard truth you've been avoiding because facing it feels overwhelming?

- Have you ever been so focused on your goals that you overlooked important realities?

Use this key to find out how to balance bold vision with a clear view of where you are now, so you can **take practical steps toward achieving your dreams**—without losing momentum or getting discouraged.

To *See Clearly and Dream Boldly*, go to page 129.

KEY #6
USE IDENTITY INSTEAD OF WILLPOWER
Align your identity with what you want.

If you've tried using willpower to make changes, you know that it usually doesn't work because it takes energy and is exhausting.

This key aligns your choices and decisions with who you truly are.

- Does success feel like something other people achieve, but not you?

- No matter how much you try to change, do you find yourself slipping back into old habits?

- Have you ever hesitated to take action because deep down, you're not sure if you're 'that kind of person'?

Trying to force yourself to take the right actions is a constant uphill battle—but **what if success could feel natural?**

This key shifts your focus from what you do to who you are, so **the right choices become effortless, sustainable**, and aligned with the future you want to create.

Start on page 153.

KEY #7
TRANSFORM PAIN INTO POWER
Turn struggle into strength and growth.

Feeling overwhelmed or afraid of failure? It's natural to want to avoid pain but ignoring it doesn't make it go away—it just keeps you stuck.

- Do you do things to avoid discomfort or challenges because they feel too overwhelming?
- When challenges appear, do they feel like roadblocks instead of opportunities for growth?
- Have you ever looked back on a tough situation and realized it actually made you stronger?

This key helps you recognize pain as a signal, not an obstacle, so you can uncover what it's really telling you and address the root cause so you can **turn problems into opportunities for growth and resilience.**

Transform Pain Into Power starts on page 175.

KEY #8
TURN CHALLENGE INTO CHOICE
Own your responses and take control of your future.

You can't always control what happens—but you can always control how you respond.

When life throws obstacles in your path, it's easy to feel helpless, stuck, or frustrated. But events, circumstances, and others don't have to control what happens—your response does.

- Do you feel like external circumstances control your success and happiness?

- Are you reacting to problems more than intentionally choosing how to handle them?

- When things don't go your way, do you find yourself blaming outside circumstances?

Use this key to shift from reacting to choosing so you can take ownership of your actions, **turn setbacks into opportunities**, and move forward with confidence.

Start on page 193.

UNLOCK YOUR BREAKTHROUGH
5 Questions to Start Thriving Now

Before moving forward, take a moment to reflect. The insights you've gained so far are only powerful if you apply them.

These five questions will help you uncover hidden obstacles, clarify where you are, and identify the best place to begin.

There's no right or wrong answer—just honest reflection.

1. **Which of the eight keys resonates with you the most right now, and why?**
   What challenge, habit, or mindset shift do you feel most drawn to working on first?

2. **What "rocks" have been weighing you down without you realizing it?**
   Are there hidden obstacles—limiting beliefs, old habits, or unhelpful thought patterns—that have been making progress harder for you?

3. **How have your past decisions shaped where you are today?**
   Looking back, can you see moments where your choices either moved you forward or kept you stuck? What can you learn from them?

4. **What's one area of your life where you're ready to stop reacting and start choosing?**
   Where do you tend to feel powerless or stuck? How can you take back control by making intentional choices?

5. **If you fully embraced these keys, how would your life be different a year from now?**
   Imagine your future self after applying these principles—what changes do you see? How would you feel?

MEET THE FOUR FRIENDS

You're the average of the five people you spend the most time with. – Jim Rohn

Think about the four people <u>you</u> spend the most time with.

Are they lifting you up, challenging you to grow, and pushing you toward success? Or are they keeping you stuck, reinforcing doubts, and making it harder to move forward?

Who you surround yourself with shapes your life more than you might realize.

The people closest to you influence your thoughts, decisions, and actions—often without you even noticing. Spend time with people who push you to grow, and you'll naturally become better because you want to fit into the group.

But if you're surrounded by negativity, doubt, or complacency, once again you will naturally seek to fit into your peer group.

That's why **one of the fastest ways to change your life is to be intentional about who you spend time with.**

The good news?

You get to decide who you associate with.

This idea of surrounding yourself with the right people is the very reason why Sarah, Michael, Emma, and Jack get together.

They know the value of having friends who not only care about them but also push them to become the best versions of themselves.

Each of them brings something unique to the group and, together, they've created a circle of support and accountability.

They don't just meet to chat about their lives; they gather to help each other face challenges, stay motivated, and take responsibility for their actions.

Sarah, for example, is driven but often worries about her choices, and she benefits from her friends' encouragement to face her fears head-on.

Michael is calm and thoughtful, always offering the kind of advice that helps his friends see their problems from a new perspective.

Meet The Four Friends

Emma is compassionate and always knows when to give someone a nudge in the right direction, pushing her friends to take action when they're stuck.

And then there's Jack, who brings his straightforward, no-nonsense attitude to every conversation, reminding the group to focus on solutions rather than excuses.

They've each faced struggles, setbacks, and moments of doubt. But together, they help each other stay strong, think bigger, and keep taking steps toward success.

WHO'S IN <u>YOUR</u> CIRCLE?

Thriving isn't just about what you do—it's also about *who you surround yourself with.* The right people challenge you, support you, and help you grow. The wrong people can hold you back without you even realizing it.

Sarah, Michael, Emma, and Jack have built a circle that lifts them higher.

Now it's your turn to reflect on your own relationships.

These five questions will help you evaluate who's in your corner and how your environment is shaping your success.

There are no right or wrong answers—just honest reflection. Let's dive in.

1. **Who are the five people you spend the most time with, and how do they influence your thoughts, actions, and mindset?**
   Are they helping you grow, or are they reinforcing doubts, bad habits, or negativity?

2. **When you face a challenge, who do you turn to first—and why?**
   Does this person help you find solutions and move forward, or do they keep you stuck in the problem?

3. **Do you have a friend like Sarah, Michael, Emma, or Jack in your life?**
   Who encourages you, offers wisdom, pushes you out of your comfort zone, or keeps you accountable? If not, where could you find people like this?

4. **Are there relationships in your life that drain your energy or keep you from becoming your best self?**
   What boundaries or changes could help you protect your growth?

5. **How can you be a better friend to the people who support and challenge you?**
   Great relationships are a two-way street—what can you do to bring more value, encouragement, and accountability to your circle?

Meet The Four Friends

THE MASTER KEY

GET STARTED KEEP GOING

Let's begin with the Master Key—*Get Started, Keep Going*—because without action, nothing else works.

This is the key that **unlocks all the others** by putting your ideas, insights, and intentions into motion.

No matter how powerful the other keys are, **they only work if you use them**—and that starts right here.

You can understand every principle in this book, but **if you don't get started and keep going, nothing changes.**

That's what makes this the Master Key.

It's the one that turns potential into progress. It's what transforms ideas into results. And it's where thriving truly begins.

It doesn't matter if you're not totally ready, if the timing isn't perfect, or if you're not sure exactly how it's going to turn out.

Action is what moves you forward.

Get Started
Keep Going

Even a small step—especially a small step—has the power to break the cycle of hesitation and create momentum.

Think of this key as your personal green light. Whatever it is you've been waiting to start... start it.

And once you begin, keep going.

Momentum builds confidence.

Progress fuels clarity.

And consistency leads to transformation.

THE MASTER KEY MOMENT

The storm outside was in full swing, streaking rain across the windows of Common Grounds Café and rattling the windchimes just outside the door.

Inside, the warmth of fresh coffee and the familiar chatter made the corner table feel like a small island of calm—at least for most of them.

Michael, however, was staring blankly at his untouched latte.

Jack noticed first. "You okay over there? You look like someone canceled your birthday."

Michael gave a weak laugh. "Honestly? I just feel stuck. I keep saying I'm going to launch my coaching business. I've got notebooks full of ideas, color-coded plans, even a spreadsheet of dream clients. But here I am. Still talking about it. Still doing… nothing."

Emma looked up from her tea. "Nothing? Come on, you've been planning for months."

"Exactly," Michael said. "Planning. Preparing. Tweaking. But I haven't actually done anything that matters. No clients. No website. No outreach. Just a lot of… thinking."

Sarah leaned in gently. "Michael, can I ask you something? Are you waiting to feel ready before you start?"

Michael nodded. "Yeah. I mean, I want to get it *right*. If I launch too early and mess it up—"

"Let me stop you right there," Jack said, cutting in with a smile. "That's like standing at the edge of a pool, waiting to be a good swimmer before you get wet. It doesn't work that way."

Michael smirked. "So what? Just dive in and hope for the best?"

Emma leaned forward. "No, not hope. *Action*. That's the Master Key. Get started—keep going. You can't steer a parked car, and you can't build momentum without moving."

Sarah added, "You've done the prep. You've got the vision. Now it's about doing something that actually counts. Even one tiny step changes the game."

Michael was quiet for a moment, chewing on their words. The rain softened outside, as if pausing for dramatic effect.

"Alright," he said slowly. "I'll send one message. Just one. There's a woman on my list I know would be a perfect fit. I'll offer her a free first session."

Jack grinned. "Now *that's* movement."

"You don't need to see the whole path," Emma said. "Just take the next step. And then the next. That's how this works."

Michael pulled out his phone, fingers hovering over the screen for a second before he started typing. "Okay. I'm doing it. No overthinking. No rewriting. Just hitting send."

He tapped the screen, then looked up. "Done."

Sarah raised her mug. "To starting."

Jack followed. "And to keeping going."

The group clinked cups as the wind outside settled into a soft hush. In that small, rainy café, something important had shifted—not just in Michael's life, but in his mindset. He wasn't waiting anymore.

He had started.

And that changed everything.

FEELING STUCK:
WHEN YOU WANT TO MOVE FORWARD BUT CAN'T

Let's start with something real—because if you're here, you've probably felt it before.

That frustrating feeling of wanting more for your life... but not knowing how to make it happen.

You have dreams, goals, or even just a sense that things *could* be better.

You're not lazy, unmotivated, or uninterested.

You care.

You want to improve. You want to grow. But instead of making progress, **you feel stuck**—like something's holding you in place.

Maybe it's the fear of doing it wrong.

Maybe it's overwhelm—there's so much to fix, you don't know where to begin.

Or maybe it's that quiet inner voice that says, *"You're not ready yet."* Or *"You're not good enough."*

Whatever the reason, the result is the same: you're waiting.

Waiting to feel more confident. Waiting for the right time. Waiting for life to slow down.

And that wait? It starts to feel permanent.

If you've ever been there, you're not alone.

I've been there too.

There was a point in my life—years into running my business—when things looked great on the outside, but I felt completely stuck on the inside. I had clients, income, and a schedule full of meetings... but I was spinning my wheels.

Everything I was doing felt like "activity," but none of it seemed to be moving me forward. And sometimes I couldn't do anything at all.

I remember sitting at my desk late one night, staring at my to-do list that never seemed to shrink. I felt exhausted—not just physically, but mentally.

It was like I was treading water in a sea of responsibilities, knowing I wasn't actually getting anywhere.

And underneath it all was this quiet frustration... because deep down, I knew I was capable of more—I just couldn't figure out how to break free.

What helped me break out of that stuck place wasn't some dramatic moment—it was a small shift.

Discovery of The Master Key

I started using the "Master Key" without realizing it: I picked one small thing that really mattered and did it. Then I did another.

Get Started
Keep Going

I stopped trying to overhaul my entire business and instead I broke it down into small pieces and I did one – then another.

I got started and kept going.

And slowly, things began to change.

I got clarity. I found my stride again.

But it all started with taking one small step and building upon it.

WHEN YOU KNOW WHAT TO DO... BUT STILL DON'T DO IT

This isn't about a lack of desire or potential. It's about the invisible weight of hesitation, fear, and uncertainty that makes taking the first step feel harder than it should.

And here's the really frustrating part: **you might even know exactly what needs to change—and still not do anything about it.**

You can read all the books, make all the plans, even visualize the outcome... and still stay stuck.

Not because you don't want change, but because you haven't yet used the one thing that makes all the difference:
Action.

That's why this isn't just another key.

It's the Master Key.

Because until you take action—until you get started and keep going—**none of the other keys can unlock the change you want to see.**

WHAT SHOULD YOU DO FIRST? START RIGHT WHERE YOU ARE

If you're feeling stuck, unsure, or overwhelmed—take a breath. You don't need to have everything figured out right now. You don't need a five-year plan or a perfect strategy.

You just need to take one small step.

Not a leap. Not a complete reinvention. Just a single, doable action that tells your brain, *"I'm moving forward now."*

It could be writing down one thing you want to change.

It could be sending that email you've been putting off.

It could be standing up, stretching, and saying out loud, *"I'm ready to get unstuck."*

Action creates momentum. And momentum makes everything easier.

You don't need to wait for motivation. You don't need to wait until you "feel ready."
Readiness comes from doing—not the other way around.

So ask yourself:

What's one small thing I can do right now that will move me forward?

And then... do it.

Right now.

Don't overthink it.

Don't judge it.

That's how it starts. That's how everything starts.

And that small step you take today?

You've broken the cycle of stuckness and it's the moment you begin to take your power back.

Let's keep going—you've already begun.

GET STARTED - KEEP GOING: THE MASTER KEY IN ACTION

Once you've taken that first small step, you've broken the cycle of stuckness—and that's huge. But to really build momentum and create lasting change, **you need a few more steps to keep going.**

Let's walk through them together—step by step, simple and doable.

And to bring it all to life, meet Leah, who, like many of us, knew she wanted more from her life but didn't know how to get started.

Step 1: Choose One Clear Goal

When <u>everything</u> feels like it needs to change, it's easy to get overwhelmed and do nothing. So instead of trying to fix everything at once, **pick one thing to focus on.**

Just one.

Leah had a notebook full of ideas—start a business, get in shape, improve her confidence—but all that ambition was weighing her down.

So she chose one clear goal: start a simple morning routine to feel more in control of her day.

What to do: Write down one thing you want to work on this week. Don't worry if it feels small.

Small and specific beats big and vague every time.

Step 2: Break It Down Into Tiny Steps

Big goals often hide behind small steps. If it feels too big, it probably needs to be broken down.

Instead of "create the perfect morning routine," Leah started with just one step: *wake up 15 minutes earlier and drink a glass of water.* That was it. Simple, doable, and repeatable.

What to do: Take your goal and break it into the smallest first step possible. Then just do that—**no pressure to do it all. Just start.**

Step 3: Create a Simple Habit Loop

The key to keeping momentum is consistency. Not perfection—**consistency.** Link your new action to something you already do every day.

Leah tied her new habit to something she already did: brushing her teeth. As soon as she finished brushing, she poured a glass of water and opened her planner.

Same trigger, same action, every day.

What to do: Pick an existing habit (waking up, brushing teeth, making coffee), and attach your new action to it. This makes it easier to stick with, even when life gets busy.

Step 4: Track Progress (Not Perfection)

Progress isn't about doing it perfectly—it's about doing it *more often than not.*

What gets tracked gets reinforced.

Leah used a sticky note calendar. Every time she followed through on her small routine, she marked an "X." It wasn't fancy, but it gave her a quick, visible way to see her wins adding up.

What to do: Use a notebook, app, or even a sticky note to track your progress. Celebrate every "yes"—and if you miss a day? Don't start over. Just start again.

Step 5: Adjust as You Go

Your journey won't be a straight line. That's okay. Life will interrupt you. You'll miss days. You might hit a wall. **What matters most is that you keep going.**

After a stressful week at work, Leah skipped her routine for three days.

Old Leah might've quit right there. But instead, she gave herself some grace, shortened her routine, and got back on track. And that's when she realized—she was finally becoming the person she wanted to be.

What to do: When life throws you off, don't beat yourself up. Ask, *"How can I make this easier or simpler?"* Then take the next step forward—however small it needs to be.

Step 6: Reflect and Recommit

Every week, **check in with yourself.** What's working? What needs adjusting?

Reflection turns action into insight—and insight keeps you moving forward with purpose instead of slipping back into a cycle of stuckness.

After 30 days, Leah looked back and realized how far she'd come. She was more focused, calmer in the mornings, and—most importantly—**more in control.** Her success wasn't flashy. But it was *real.*

What to do: Ask yourself:

- What's working well?
- Is anything getting in my way?

- What's one small adjustment I can make to keep going?

THE BOTTOM LINE: YOU'VE GOT THIS

Getting unstuck isn't about massive action—it's about **consistent, imperfect action** that aligns with who you want to become.

So take your first step.

Then another.

And another.

And remember—**you don't have to get it perfect. You just have to keep going.**

You're not stuck.

You're just getting started.

NOW THAT YOU'RE MOVING— LET'S UNLOCK WHAT COMES NEXT

By using the Master Key—Get Started, Keep Going—you've already taken the most important step: you're in motion. That feeling of being stuck?

It starts to fade the moment you take action, even if it's small.

But momentum alone isn't enough. To keep growing, thriving, and building the life you truly want, you need direction. And that's where the next key comes in.

Because the truth is, **not all action is created equal.**

Some steps move you forward. Others keep you busy but stuck. If you want to build a life that lasts, you need to make decisions that support the future you're working toward—not just today's comfort.

That's why **our first key is all about making better choices**—choices that don't just feel good now, but create real results down the road.

Let's unlock your next step with Key #1: Future-Proof Your Decisions.

Get Started
Keep Going

KEY #1

FUTURE-PROOF YOUR DECISIONS

The choices you make today create your future—this key shows you how to think beyond quick wins and make decisions that set you up for lasting success.

Imagine you're planting a tree.

You carefully choose the spot, prepare the soil, and envision the shade it will one day provide.

You know the tree won't grow overnight, but every decision you make now—where to plant it, how to nurture it—will shape its future.

That's the essence of making big picture decisions: thinking beyond today's quick wins to build a foundation for long-term success.

In this chapter, we'll explore how shifting your focus to the long term can transform the way you approach your goals and challenges.

It's about looking past the immediate distractions and short-term benefits to ask yourself: What will truly matter a year, five years, or even ten years from now?

By learning to think this way, you'll not only set yourself up for greater achievements, but you'll also feel more grounded and confident in the choices you make today.

The decisions you make today ripple out far into your future, whether you realize it or not.

By using a short time frame to make an important decision, you're setting yourself up to be blindsided by the consequences of your choice.

Let's join the friends at the Common Grounds Café…

THE NEW JOB

The sun was beginning to dip behind the row of brick buildings lining the street, casting long shadows over the Common Grounds Café where Sarah, Michael, and Emma met for their regular catch-up.

Jack was out of town on business, but the familiar trio settled into their usual corner table, ready to dive into conversation.

It had become a ritual over the years—ever since college when the four of them would stay up late in the library, dreaming about where life would take them.

The Common Grounds was their favorite spot, with its mismatched chairs and the comforting scent of freshly brewed coffee. Today, however, the usual easy banter was missing. Sarah sat slumped in her seat, staring at her untouched latte, her thoughts miles away.

Sarah was the kind of person who always seemed to have it all together—organized, driven, and meticulous.

She had climbed the corporate ladder quickly in her marketing job at 366 Solar, earning herself a steady paycheck and a good reputation.

But recently, something had shifted.

The spark she once had for her work was starting to dim, and it was showing in the way she was hunched over the table now, her brows knitted in thought.

Emma, always the most empathetic of the group, was the first to notice.

She had an artist's heart and a free spirit, often filling her days with painting and writing while juggling freelance design work.

She reached across the table and touched Sarah's hand. "Hey, you look like you're carrying the weight of the world today," she said softly. "What's going on?"

Michael, on the other hand, was analytical and practical, with a knack for strategy. He worked as a consultant, where he helped businesses streamline their operations.

He leaned back in his chair, looking at Sarah with curiosity. "Yeah, spill it," he added. "You've been out of it since you walked in."

Sarah glanced up, a flicker of uncertainty crossing her face. "It's just…I've got this huge decision to make, and I'm not sure if I'm thinking about it the right way," she said, her voice trailing off.

Michael raised an eyebrow. "Sounds serious. What kind of decision?"

Sarah took a deep breath, finally letting her guard down. "I got offered a job at this startup," she began, a hint of excitement creeping into her voice. "It's a COO position. The team's small but really talented, and they're working on some exciting stuff. The salary is decent, and there's equity involved… but there's a catch. They need me to decide by Friday, and I'd have to leave my job at 366 in two weeks."

Emma's eyes widened, and she leaned forward eagerly. "Wow, Sarah, that sounds incredible! You've always talked about wanting to be a bigger part of something. Why the hesitation?"

Sarah's fingers traced the rim of her coffee cup nervously. "I know, and that's what makes it so hard. I've been in this stable job for five years now. I've built a good life there… but lately, I've felt like I'm just coasting. The startup seems risky—like, really risky. They're still pre-profit, and if things go south, I could be out of a job in less than a year. Part of me wants to dive in because it's exciting, but the other part is terrified of what could happen."

Michael gave a knowing nod. "So, they're pushing you to make a quick decision?"

Sarah nodded. "They want an answer by Friday," she said with a sigh. "I'm trying to weigh the pros and cons, but I keep going back and forth."

Emma tapped her chin thoughtfully, her voice softening with concern. "It sounds like you're focusing a lot on the immediate benefits, like the salary bump and the thrill of joining a startup. But have you thought about what this means for your future? Where do you see yourself in five, ten years?"

Sarah's brow furrowed as she let Emma's question sink in. "I mean...I haven't really looked that far ahead," she admitted. "I've been so focused on the short-term—the excitement, the new title, the pay increase. I guess I've been avoiding thinking about whether it's actually the right fit for where I want to be long-term and the consequences of what will happen if the company fails."

Michael leaned forward, his tone firm but kind. "Look, I get it. A new opportunity can feel like a shot of adrenaline. I've made decisions in the past that seemed like the right move in the moment—projects that paid well or had a lot of buzz. But then I'd look up a year later and realize I'd drifted away from my bigger goals. Don't just ask yourself if this is a good opportunity; ask yourself if it's a good opportunity *for you*."

Emma's expression softened as she leaned in closer. "Remember when I took that design contract with that big agency last year? It was supposed to be a dream gig, but I jumped in without thinking about whether it aligned with what I actually wanted. I got so caught up in keeping up with their demands that I forgot why I started freelancing in the first place. I was way too busy to paint anymore, and I wasn't writing... I was just stuck in the grind."

Sarah's eyes met Emma's, a glint of understanding crossing her face. "You're right," she said quietly. "I've been looking at this decision through such a narrow lens—thinking only about the next few months. But if the startup fails...or even if it doesn't, what if it takes me in a direction I don't want to go?"

Michael nodded. "Exactly. The more significant the decision, the longer you need to extend your time horizon. The question isn't just whether you can handle the risk; it's whether that risk is worth taking because it aligns with your vision and needs for the future. If you were to look back on this decision ten years from now, would you be proud of the path it put you on, or would you see it as a detour?"

Sarah took a deep breath, a new sense of clarity settling in. "You're both right," she said. "I need to think beyond the immediate benefits. It's time to ask myself where I actually want to end up and whether this opportunity fits into that picture."

Emma grinned, her eyes twinkling. "Now you're talking. Sometimes you've just got to step back and see the bigger picture. It's not always about saying 'yes' to what's exciting, but saying 'yes' to what's right for your future."

Michael raised his coffee cup, a small smile forming. "To choosing the path that leads you where you actually want to go."

Sarah clinked her cup against his, feeling a newfound resolve. "Cheers to that. I'm going to figure out where I really want to be in ten years, and I'm going to make my decision with that in mind."

As Sarah walked out of the café that evening, she felt lighter.

It wasn't just about the excitement anymore.

It was about her life—her goals, her future. She realized she had the power to shape it, but only if she made decisions that truly aligned with the person she wanted to become.

It was time to extend her time frame and think bigger.

THE LURE OF IMMEDIATE GRATIFICATION

We live in a world that's wired for instant results.

Hungry? DoorDash will have food at your door in 15 minutes.

Need something new? Amazon can deliver it by tomorrow.

Want entertainment? You can stream anything instantly, anytime.

We don't have to wait for much anymore, and that's changed the way we think and created some unfortunate side effects.

If something isn't happening now, it can feel like it's not worth our attention.

This same mindset creeps into how we make decisions. It's easy to focus on what's convenient, what feels good in the moment, or what solves the problem right now.

And sometimes, short-term decisions are fine. Not everything needs a five-year plan.

But here's where it gets tricky: short-term decisions have a way of turning into long-term consequences.

- Saying yes to something easy today can make life harder tomorrow.
- A quick fix can create bigger problems down the road.
- Choosing what feels good now can keep you stuck in the same place later.

The good news?

You don't have to sacrifice today for the future—you just need to think beyond the moment.

The key is learning to pause, step back, and ask yourself: Is this choice taking me where I want to go?

You don't have to have everything figured out.

But when you start thinking ahead—even just a little—you give yourself a huge advantage.

THE LONG-TERM CONSEQUENCES YOU DIDN'T SEE COMING

Here's the tricky part: **decisions that seem small and insignificant today can have a huge impact down the road.**

Think about it like planting seeds.

A bad decision is like planting a weed. At first, it might seem harmless, maybe even unnoticeable. But over time, that weed can grow into something that chokes out the life of everything good in your garden.

The results of short-term thinking often don't show up immediately, but when they do, they can hit hard.

Your health is a good example.

If you make daily decisions based primarily on what's easiest in the moment—whether that's not exercising or eating fast food way too often—you probably won't notice any major consequences right away.

But these decisions add up and, a few years down the line, you find yourself battling preventable health issues that are much harder or impossible to reverse.

The same goes for your finances.

Buying what you want now without thinking about the long-term impact on your savings or retirement might feel great in the present, but future-you will eventually be the one who has to deal with the fallout.

In your career, short-term thinking might lead you to hop from job to job, never committing to a long-term goal or skill development.

Sure, a new position might offer a bigger paycheck or more perks, but if you're not thinking about where it's leading you in the next five or ten years, you could find yourself with a resume full of short stints and a reputation as someone who lacks direction.

THE POWER OF SMALL CHOICES OVER TIME

Here's something else to think about: **the impact of one small choice might be harmless by itself, but the cumulative effect of repeating it over time can lead to significant problems.**

Here's an example we can all relate to: Opting for that daily $5 coffee instead of brewing your own might feel like a minor indulgence, but over a year, it adds up to nearly

$2,000—money that could have gone toward a vacation or an emergency fund.

Or consider skipping your evening walk in favor of scrolling on your phone. It's just one evening, right? But over time, it chips away at your fitness and energy levels.

Now, let's flip the script.

Imagine making small, positive choices instead—like brewing your coffee at home, or taking that short walk every evening.

These seemingly minor habits build up, creating a ripple effect that leads to healthier finances and more energy.

The key is recognizing patterns early and making adjustments that align with your long-term goals.

Each small decision adds up, shaping the direction of your life, many times without you noticing it.

What small decisions can you start (or stop) making today to set yourself up for the success and fulfillment you truly want?"

THE BIGGER THE DECISION
THE LONGER THE TIME FRAME

Here's the important thing:

The more significant the decision, the more crucial it becomes to think beyond the immediate future.

When you're making choices that could affect your career, relationships, health, or long-term happiness, a short-term focus usually isn't long enough.

Future-Proof Your Decisions

Major decisions come with major consequences—both positive and negative.

Because these decisions can shape the trajectory of your life for years, even decades, it's essential to look past the here and now and consider how today's choice could impact your future self.

Think about it like this: if you're deciding whether to meet a friend for lunch today, the long-term consequences are minimal, so you don't need a very long time frame for the decision.

But if you're deciding whether to make a large financial investment, accept a job offer, or end a significant relationship, these decisions can have ripple effects that extend far beyond tomorrow, next week, or even next year.

The decisions you make in these pivotal moments will set the course for your business, career, personal growth, and overall well-being.

If you don't give these choices the time and consideration they deserve, you're gambling with your future—and the stakes are high.

But when you deliberately take the time to project the consequences of your decisions into the future, you're more likely to make choices that support your goals and values.

When you weigh the potential long-term impact of a decision, you give yourself the opportunity to **make choices that not only serve your immediate needs but also lay the foundation for a future you'll be proud of.**

This kind of big picture thinking makes sure that you're not just reacting to the present but actively building the life you want for the years ahead.

After all, thriving isn't about quick fixes, it's about building a future that brings sustained joy and fulfillment.

HOW TO ESCAPE THE SHORT-TERM DECISION TRAP

As you can see, it's easy to make important decisions based on short-term benefits because immediate needs and desires often demand your attention.

Recognizing this tendency is the first step toward shifting your focus and reclaiming control over your choices.

So, how can you turn things around?

It starts with determining which decisions you make today will have the most impact on your future.

Ask yourself, "How will this choice affect me in one year? Five years? Ten years?"

By expanding your time frame, you'll make better, more thoughtful decisions that will set you up for long-term success and happiness.

As you make your decisions, remember that **many times immediate gratification comes at the expense of long-term satisfaction.**

When faced with an important choice that will have a long-term impact, delay your decision for a moment and consider the potential long term outcomes.

Will that impulse buy bring you joy in the future, or will it create a pile of regret?

Will staying in a comfortable but dead-end job serve you in the long run, or is it time to take a risk and pursue something more meaningful?

Like Sarah, it's important to lengthen your time frame and think of the big picture to make sure you are making the best decision possible.

HOW DO YOU MAKE DECISIONS?

So, know that you know the importance of making big decisions using a bigger picture, longer time frame here are some questions you can use to find out how you tend to make decisions:

1. **Am I prioritizing immediate gratification over long-term goals?**
   Example: Am I choosing short-term pleasure, like impulse spending or unhealthy habits, without considering how it will affect my future?

2. **Have I thought about how this decision will impact me five or ten years from now?**
   Example: In making career choices or financial commitments, do I take into account where I want to be in the long term?

3. **Am I avoiding difficult conversations or decisions because they're uncomfortable now, even though they might improve my future?**
   Example: Do I avoid addressing issues in relationships or work that could have long-term consequences?

4. **Do I tend to choose what feels good in the moment, even when I know it might have negative consequences later?**
   Example: Am I making choices like eating poorly or not saving money, knowing it could hurt my health or financial stability later?

5. **Am I frequently changing jobs, goals, or relationships without considering how that instability affects my future?**
   Example: Am I hopping from one thing to another, never thinking about how it builds—or erodes—my long-term progress?

6. **Am I neglecting to invest in my personal growth or skills because the payoff isn't immediate?**
   Example: Am I avoiding learning new skills, saving, or working on my health because I don't see an instant benefit?

7. **Do I spend more time thinking about short-term pleasures (like vacations, shopping, or entertainment) than I do planning for my future (retirement, career growth, or personal development)?**
   (Example: Is my focus primarily on short-term fun

rather than on securing my long-term success or happiness?)

HOW TO KNOW THE RIGHT TIME FRAME FOR A DECISION

Most decisions don't require big picture thinking, so when faced with a decision, it's important to determine whether it requires long-term thinking and how to set an appropriate time frame.

Take a few minutes and ask yourself these five key questions to know whether the decision should be made with a long-term perspective:

Think About The Impact

1. **Does this decision have long-lasting consequences?**
   If the impact of the decision will be felt for years (e.g., buying a home, changing careers, committing to a relationship), it requires a longer time horizon.

2. **Is this decision related to a critical area of life (health, finances, career, relationships)?**
   Major areas of life typically demand long-term thinking because these outcomes shape your future in meaningful ways.

3. **Will the decision affect other people or involve commitments to them?**
   If your choice impacts others (e.g., family, colleagues, partners), or if it involves promises or contracts, thinking long-term is crucial.

4. **What is the risk of regret if the decision doesn't work out over time?**
   If you're likely to regret a decision in a few years if it goes wrong, it's a strong indicator that you need to think further ahead.

5. **Can I reverse the decision easily or is it hard to undo?**
   Decisions that are difficult or impossible to reverse (e.g., signing a lease, taking on debt, choosing a career path) need to be made on a longer time horizon.

The more you answer "yes" to these five questions, the stronger the indication that you need to look at the big picture.

Determine Whether the Time Frame is Long Enough

If you've determined that a decision requires long-term thinking, use these guidelines to ensure the length of the time frame is long enough:

1. **Consider the life cycle of the decision.**
   Think about how long the decision will remain relevant. For example, if you're buying a car, the time frame should reflect how long you expect to use the car and its future costs, not just the immediate need.

2. **Think about where you want to be in 1, 5, and 10 years.**
   Evaluate whether this decision aligns with your long-term goals. If the decision doesn't positively contribute to where you want to be in those time frames, reconsider it or adjust the plan.

3. **Anticipate potential challenges or changes over time.**
   Imagine how this decision will hold up under different future scenarios. Will this choice still work if your job changes, your health changes, or the market shifts?

4. **Balance flexibility and commitment.**
   Ensure your time frame allows for some flexibility in case circumstances change, but also that you're committed to seeing the decision through for a reasonable period. Avoid locking yourself into long-term commitments without a way to adapt.

5. **Factor in delayed benefits or long-term growth.**
   If the benefits of your decision will take time to materialize (e.g., education, investments, building a career), choose a time frame that gives those benefits a chance to unfold fully.

6. **Consult with others who have experience with similar decisions.**
   Sometimes we underestimate how long a decision's consequences will last. Seek advice from others who have been through similar choices to get a realistic idea of the appropriate time horizon.

Quick Decision Checklist:

- ☑ **Impact duration:** How long will this decision affect me?
- ☑ **Reversibility:** Can I undo this decision easily if needed?

- ☑ **Alignment with long-term goals:** Does this choice support my 5, 10, or 20-year vision?
- ☑ **Anticipated changes:** Will this decision still make sense if my circumstances change?
- ☑ **Delayed outcomes:** Am I prepared to wait for the results of this choice, or am I expecting instant rewards?

When you use these guidelines, you'll gain clarity, confidence, and the peace of knowing your decisions are building the future you truly want.

TRACK YOUR DECISIONS

Tracking your decision-making patterns is one of the best ways to see if you are making decisions on the best time frame and it can be a game-changer.

It's like having a personal roadmap to help you make better, more intentional choices. Here's how to start:

Keep a Decision Journal

Imagine a diary, but for your decisions!

Jot down what choices you made, why you made them, and how they turned out. Did your decision bring you closer to your goals? This simple habit can reveal a lot about your thought process.

Example: "Ordered takeout because I was tired. Next time, I'll plan quick meals in advance."

Look Back to Move Forward

Make a list of past choices and reflect on them. What worked? What didn't? Look for the impact of repeated small decisions can help you make better ones in the future.

Spot the Instant Gratification Traps

We've all been there—choosing what feels good right now over what's better later. Pay attention to these moments and replace the impulse with healthier, more productive habits.

Rate Your Decisions

Give each decision a score from 1 to 5 based on how well it supports your bigger goals. Over time, you'll notice patterns and areas for growth.

Celebrate Your Wins

Don't forget to cheer yourself on! Every time you make a thoughtful, long-term decision, take a moment to appreciate your progress.

When you use these steps, you'll build stronger decision-making habits and feel more confident about the path you're creating.

Remember, every small choice counts—and with the right mindset, you're unstoppable!

THINK AND THRIVE:
5 QUESTIONS TO FUTURE-PROOF YOUR SUCCESS

The decisions you make today are planting the seeds for your future—but **are you planting trees that will thrive, or weeds that will take over?**

It's easy to get caught up in what feels good or convenient right now, but taking a moment to think ahead can save you from regret and set you up for long-term success.

These five questions will help you step back, reflect, and make choices that support the future *you* want to create.

No pressure—just honest reflection. Your future self will thank you.

1. **What's one decision you made in the past that seemed small at the time but had a big impact later?**
   Was it a good impact or a bad one? What can you learn from that experience?

2. **Are there areas of your life where you tend to make decisions based on short-term comfort instead of long-term benefit?**
   Health, finances, career, relationships—where do you catch yourself choosing what's easy now over what's best for the future?

3. **If you made decisions with your "future self" in mind, what would you do differently?**
   Imagine yourself five years from now—what choices today would make that version of you proud?

4. **What's one big decision you're facing right now? How could thinking five or ten years ahead help you make a better choice?**
   Take a step back from the moment—what long-term impact could this choice have?

5. **What's one habit or mindset shift you can start today that will set you up for success in the future?**
   Big changes aren't always necessary—sometimes, it's the small, consistent shifts that make the biggest difference over time.

THE BOTTOM LINE

Making important decisions on a time frame that's too short can lead to a life full of regret and missed opportunities, so take a few minutes to consider the benefits of shifting your thinking.

Take the long view, make choices that align with your future goals not just your immediate desires, and remember that **the small decisions you make today will shape the rest of your life.**

After all, one of the best ways to thrive is to consciously think about the life you're creating.

KEY #2

WORK SMART TO FINISH STRONG

Being busy isn't the same as being effective—this key helps you focus on what truly moves you ahead and follow through so your hard work creates real impact.

Imagine planting seeds in a garden without ever checking to see if they're growing.

You might water them carefully, pull weeds, and spend hours tending to the soil—but if you're not paying attention to the results, you could end up with a lot of effort and no harvest.

That's what happens when we confuse being busy with being productive.

Staying focused on meaningful outcomes means **shifting your attention from the busyness of activity to progress that truly matters.**

It's about asking, "What am I really trying to achieve here?" and then aligning your efforts to move closer to that goal.

The good news?

Once you start focusing on results, you'll notice **your time and energy being used more effectively**, giving you a greater sense of accomplishment and momentum.

Get ready to stop spinning your wheels and start thriving!

THE PRODUCTIVITY TRAP

It was late afternoon, and the Common Grounds Café buzzed with its usual mix of chatter and the intermittent clatter of espresso machines.

Jack was still out of town, and Sarah, Michael, and Emma were once again gathered at their favorite corner table. But today, Sarah seemed different. Her eyes were tired, and her face had a weary look that even her extra-large latte couldn't overcome.

She scrolled aimlessly on her phone, only looking up occasionally to nod as Michael and Emma talked.

Emma leaned in, noticing how distracted Sarah was. "Hey, Earth to Sarah. What's up? You look like you've been pulling an all-nighter."

Sarah sighed heavily, tossing her phone onto the table.

"That's because I have been. I can't seem to catch a break. I've been working late every night, responding to emails, hopping from one meeting to another, fine-tuning presentations...I'm doing everything I'm supposed to, but it still feels like I'm running in circles."

Michael gave her a curious look. "What are you actually trying to achieve right now? I mean, what's the goal?"

"The goal?" Sarah echoed, sounding almost puzzled. "I guess...just staying on top of things. There's always something that needs my attention, and if I don't keep up, it's all going to collapse."

Emma frowned, setting down her cup. "But Sarah, are you really getting anything done, or are you just drowning in busywork? There's a big difference."

Sarah's brow furrowed as she took a moment to think. "What do you mean? I'm working my tail off. Isn't that supposed to be enough?"

Michael shook his head gently. "Not if you're just doing stuff for the sake of doing it, doing the wrong things, or starting a project only to abandon it for something else before it's finished. I used to be just like that—answering emails the second they hit my inbox, filling my calendar with meetings, and constantly tweaking little details. Starting things and not finishing them. I convinced myself I was being productive because I was always busy. But in reality, I was just spinning my wheels."

"I get that," Emma said. "It's like the time I spent weeks planning every tiny detail of my new project launch. I made color-coded charts, endless spreadsheets, and had meetings with people who didn't even need to be involved. It felt good to stay busy, but when I finally looked up, I realized I hadn't made any actual progress toward getting the project off the ground. I was mistaking the thrill of activity for actual results."

Sarah sighed again, deeper this time. "You know, I've been feeling that way for a while, but I kept telling myself, 'At least I'm doing something.' I just didn't want to admit that I don't really know what I'm working toward. I'm putting out fires and staying busy, but I'm not sure it's leading anywhere."

Michael leaned in closer, his voice calm but firm. "You're stuck in the productivity trap, Sarah. When we confuse activity with results, we end up filling our days with things that don't actually matter. It feels safer than facing the tough question of whether what we're doing is meaningful. But that's how you can accidentally waste your life."

Emma nodded enthusiastically. "Exactly. You need to start asking yourself if what you're doing is actually moving you toward something you care about. If it's not, then you're just wasting time."

Sarah looked at them, a mixture of realization and frustration crossing her face. "I think I've been avoiding that question because I didn't want to admit that all this busyness is just... empty. I thought as long as I kept my schedule packed, I was doing okay. But I'm exhausted, and I'm not even sure why."

Michael gave a reassuring smile. "You're not alone, and it's not too late to turn it around. My mentor taught me to start small. Pick one goal—something that really matters to you—and focus on actually completing it. You don't have to fill every minute with tasks to be productive."

Emma raised her cup in a toast. "Here's to fewer distractions, more direction, and completing the next thing you start."

Sarah picked up her coffee, feeling a spark of hope and determination. "To cutting the noise and focusing on what actually counts. I'm done being busy for the sake of being busy."

As Sarah walked out of the café that day, she felt a shift in perspective.

For the first time in a long time, she wasn't going to measure her productivity by how packed her schedule was. Instead, she would focus on actions that truly mattered and completing the things she started.

It was time to escape the productivity trap and start moving toward something real.

THE COMFORT OF BEING BUSY

Staying busy can feel great—it gives you that satisfying sense of accomplishment as you check items off your to-do list.

But imagine how much more fulfilling it is to channel that energy into tasks that truly move the needle toward your goals.

Not all action is equal, and that's a good thing!

Some actions pack more punch, moving you closer to your goals faster and with greater impact. It's like the difference between scattering seeds randomly and planting them in fertile soil with care.

Both involve effort, but one is far more likely to grow into something meaningful.

By focusing your energy on purposeful, high-impact actions, you ensure that your time is well spent and your progress is tangible.

The beauty of this approach?

It helps you work smarter, not harder, and leaves you feeling accomplished and energized as you move toward the results that truly matter.

Take Brian, for example.

He dedicates hours to organizing his email inbox and attending meetings, filling his day with activity. But when he shifts his focus to activities that grow his small business—like connecting with potential clients or refining his services—his progress skyrockets.

Then there's Jenna, who loves reading self-help books. She felt proud of the knowledge she was gaining, but when she started actively applying what she learned, her life began to transform. The ideas in those books became real changes in her daily routine, helping her achieve her goals faster than she ever expected.

By focusing on meaningful outcomes, Brian and Jenna discovered the power of intentional action.

When you direct your efforts toward what truly matters, you make real progress—and that's where the magic happens!

THE DIFFERENCE BETWEEN BEING BUSY AND BEING EFFECTIVE

Activity and results aren't the same, and that creates a great opportunity because it means you can achieve more by focusing your energy on what truly matters.

Instead of feeling stuck in the grind of endless tasks, you have the power to prioritize high-impact actions that bring real progress.

This distinction allows you to work smarter, not harder, and ensures your time and effort lead to meaningful outcomes.

It's freeing to know that <u>you don't have to do everything</u>—you just have to do the right things.

Being busy means doing many things, but being effective is about doing the <u>right</u> things.

When we approach our days with intention and focus, every action becomes a step toward meaningful progress.

Sometimes, we fill our schedules with tasks because we're driven to succeed, improve, or simply keep up with life's demands.

But there are other reasons too!

Maybe we enjoy the feeling of being busy—it gives us a sense of purpose and accomplishment.

Or perhaps we're trying to avoid tough decisions or uncomfortable emotions by staying preoccupied. For some, it's about seeking validation: staying busy can make us feel valuable and important.

And let's be honest, sometimes we get caught up in busy work because it's easier than tackling the bigger, more challenging tasks that really matter.

Whatever the reason, recognizing these patterns gives us the chance to refocus and align our time with what truly brings value to our lives.

By focusing on what truly aligns with our goals, we transform activity into genuine progress.

It's not about working harder or doing more; it's about directing our energy toward what matters most.

Imagine starting a new fitness routine.

Instead of wandering aimlessly around the gym for an hour, you follow a structured 30 minute plan designed to meet your specific goals. Suddenly, your workouts feel purposeful, and you start seeing real results.

When your actions are specific and carefully aligned with a meaningful outcome, magic happens.

Every step you take feels purposeful, and even small wins bring a sense of progress and fulfillment.

Instead of spreading your energy thin across countless tasks, you're laser-focused on what matters most.

It's like planting seeds in fertile soil—you know exactly where to water and nurture, so your efforts flourish.

The best part?

You start seeing real, tangible results that fuel your motivation to keep going.

Whether it's advancing in your career, building stronger relationships, or improving your health, aligning your actions with a clear goal creates momentum.

Each choice becomes a building block toward the bigger picture, and you gain confidence knowing your time and energy are creating meaningful change.

Life feels less like a chaotic race and more like a well-charted journey.

You're not just busy—you're making intentional strides toward the life you want, and that's where the true sense of accomplishment lies.

ARE ANY OF THESE KEEPING YOU BUSY?

Here are some common activities that seem like productivity, but probably aren't. Do any of these seem familiar?

Fill*ing* Your Schedule With Meetings

If you pack your calendar with meetings, you'll always feel busy, even if most of those meetings don't accomplish much. When you prioritize the right conversations and commitments, you'll accomplish more with less effort and feel a greater sense of achievement.

Working On Low-Priority Tasks First

It's tempting to start with the easier tasks to build momentum—and while that can feel good, **true progress comes from focusing on what matters most.** When you prioritize tasks that move the needle, you'll not only stay productive, but you'll also see real results that bring you closer to your goals.

Multitasking Constantly

Juggling multiple tasks can make you feel productive, but it can lead to partially finished work and scattered results. When you give your full attention to what matters most, you'll complete tasks more effectively, see better results, and feel a greater sense of accomplishment.

Not Setting Clear Goals

When you clearly define what you want to achieve, every action you take becomes more purposeful and rewarding. Instead of just staying busy, you'll focus on what truly matters, making progress that brings you closer to your goals with confidence and clarity.

Measuring Success by How Exhausted You Feel

Feeling tired at the end of the day can be a sign of hard work, but **true productivity comes from making meaningful progress, not just staying busy.**

When you focus on the right tasks, you'll end the day not just exhausted, but accomplished—knowing your efforts are moving you closer to your goals.

WHY ACTIVITY FEELS PRODUCTIVE (EVEN WHEN IT ISN'T)

As human beings we are wired to feel a sense of accomplishment from taking action, even if that action isn't the best thing to be doing.

It's easy to make the mistake of thinking, "At least I'm doing something," rather than asking whether what you're doing is moving you closer to your goals.

We often seek quick wins to feel good about ourselves, but unfortunately this leads to wasted time and missed opportunities.

For example, imagine an entrepreneur who spends all day tweaking the design of their company's website instead of focusing on getting new customers or improving the product.

The activity feels like progress because it keeps them busy and gives them a sense of control, but in reality, it doesn't get the business closer to profitability.

90% DONE IS ALMOST THERE BUT NOT DONE!

Starting new projects is exciting, isn't it?

The thrill of diving into fresh ideas, fueled by creativity and enthusiasm, feels amazing.

But **the real magic happens when you see a project through to the finish line.** That's when all your effort and energy pay off, delivering tangible results that bring a deep sense of accomplishment.

Even if you're 90% there, you're not done!

The reality is that **90% done is 0% done** because without being complete, the project isn't usable and doesn't deliver any benefit for the work you have put into it.

If you don't complete it, you have wasted all the time and energy it took to get to 90%!

The final push—the last 10%—is where the true value lies.

By completing what you start, you transform your hard work into something meaningful and impactful.

Think of a writer working on a novel.

The first few chapters are filled with inspiration, and as the story unfolds, the writer pushes through the tough parts, weaving the plot together.

By sticking with it, they hold a finished manuscript—a book ready to be shared with the world. Every hour spent writing now counts toward a real achievement.

Staying focused on completing a task brings clarity, satisfaction, and momentum.

Instead of being spread thin across too many projects, you'll enjoy the rewards of finishing strong.

Each completed project becomes a stepping stone toward bigger goals and greater confidence in your ability to succeed.

WHAT IF YOU'RE READY TO START BUT DON'T KNOW HOW?

Sometimes, the challenge isn't about being too busy or leaving things incomplete—it's about feeling unsure of where to begin.

The idea of getting started can feel overwhelming, especially when the goal seems big and distant.

But here's the good news: **every journey starts with one small step, and progress is all about breaking things down into manageable pieces.**

Take Mia, for example. She dreamed of playing the guitar and even bought a beautiful instrument, complete with online tutorials and courses.

But the big picture—becoming a confident guitarist—felt far away and intimidating. Instead of diving in, she froze, unsure of how to begin. The guitar sat untouched, and her dream felt further away each day.

The key for Mia, and for anyone feeling stuck, is to shift focus from the entire staircase to just the first step.

Break what you need to do into small steps and take the first step. If that step is still too big, continue breaking it down into smaller steps until you get one you can do.

Then, once you're started with that small step, do the next step and keep moving one step at a time.

For Mia, it was as simple as tuning her guitar and playing one chord. Each small action built momentum and gave her the confidence to keep going.

If you're feeling stuck, ask yourself: what's one small step I can take today?

It could be writing a single sentence, making one phone call, or taking a short walk. Progress doesn't usually come from giant leaps—it comes from consistent, small actions that build on each other.

When your focus is on finishing that first step, you'll find it easier to take the next one.

Little by little, you'll replace uncertainty with progress and rediscover the excitement of moving toward your goals.

Progress begins with a single step, and even the smallest action moves you closer to your goal!

HOW TO KNOW IF YOU'RE WORKING TOWARD A MEANINGFUL OUTCOME OR JUST STAYING BUSY

1. **Does this task bring me closer to a specific goal?**
   Example: Writing a draft of your presentation aligns with your goal of delivering a successful pitch. But if you continue to rewrite the draft without delivering the presentation, the time and energy is wasted.

2. **How can I measure progress on this task?**
   Example: Tracking the number of completed client follow-ups shows clear progress toward building relationships.

3. **Is this task something only I can do, or could it be delegated?**
   Example: Delegating data entry to a team member

frees you to focus on strategic planning. Hiring a freelancer or using AI to refine your website.

4. **Will completing this task have a lasting impact?**
   Example: Sending a quick email might feel productive, but creating a streamlined system for handling emails will save you time every day—making a lasting impact instead of just checking a box.

5. **Does this task align with my top priorities?**
   Example: Preparing for your performance review reflects your priority of advancing your career.

6. **Am I avoiding something more important by focusing on this task?**
   Example: Organizing your desk might feel productive, but completing your client proposal is the real priority.

By asking these questions, you'll stay focused on meaningful actions that drive results, leaving busywork behind!

HOW TO FOCUS ON WHAT REALLY MATTERS

At the end of the day, do you ever stop and wonder, "Did all that work actually bring me closer to my goals?"

That's where this guide comes in!

It's not about doing *more*; it's about doing what *matters*, and actually *completing* what you start.

Here are some simple steps and questions you can use to focus your energy on meaningful actions that lead to real results.

Let's turn all that effort into progress you can see and feel!

Define Your Outcome Clearly

Start by knowing exactly what you're working toward.
Question: What specific result do I want to achieve?
Example: Instead of "get more clients," your goal could be "sign three new clients this month."

Break Your Outcome Into Small Actionable Steps

Identify specific tasks that will move you toward your goal.
Question: What small, concrete steps can I take to make progress toward my goal?
Example: "Reach out to 10 potential clients this week" is an actionable and measurable step that leads to signing new clients.

Prioritize High-Impact Tasks

Focus on the tasks that will make the biggest difference.
Question: Which task will have the greatest impact on achieving my goal?
Example: Spending time preparing for a client pitch has more impact than organizing your inbox.

Set Measurable Milestones

Track your progress with clear benchmarks along the way.
Question: How will I know I'm making progress toward my goal?
Example: "Schedule three client calls this week" is a measurable milestone for your goal of signing clients.

Regularly Review Your Progress

Take time to reflect on what's working and adjust as needed.

Question: Are the tasks I'm completing actually moving me closer to my goal?

Example: At the end of the week, ask yourself: "Did these tasks help me sign new clients?"

Limit Distractions and Busywork

Be mindful of tasks that fill your time without contributing to your goal.

Question: Am I spending time on tasks that feel productive but don't create real progress?

Example: Spending an hour formatting your to-do list might feel productive, but it doesn't directly support your goal.

Celebrate Meaningful Wins

Acknowledge when your efforts lead to real results—it keeps you motivated!

Question: What progress have I made, and how can I celebrate my success?

Example: Signing your first new client is a milestone worth celebrating.

By asking these questions at each step, you'll stay on track, prioritize what truly matters, and ensure your efforts lead to meaningful results.

Let's turn your actions into achievements!

WORK SMARTER, ACHIEVE MORE
5 QUESTIONS TO HELP YOU FOCUS ON WHAT MATTERS

We all want to feel productive, but **are you busy, or are you actually making progress?**

These five questions will help you step back, evaluate how you're spending your time, and make sure your effort is creating real results. No guilt, no pressure—just a chance to reflect and refocus.

Ready to make every effort count? Let's dive in.

1. **At the end of the day, do you feel accomplished—or just exhausted?**
   Are you making meaningful progress, or just keeping yourself busy?

2. **What's one thing you've been spending time on that isn't really moving you forward?**
   Are there tasks that feel productive but aren't actually helping you reach your goals?

3. **When you plan your day, do you prioritize the most important tasks—or just the easiest ones?**
   Are you tackling high-impact work first, or getting stuck in small, low-value tasks?

4. **Will what you're working on today still matter a month or a year from now?**
   Are you focusing on work that has lasting impact, or just reacting to what's urgent?

5. **If you were going to only focus on three things this week, what would they be?**
   What truly matters, and how can you eliminate distractions to make it happen?

THE BOTTOM LINE

Focusing on meaningful results is the second key to building the life you truly want. When you align your actions with clear goals, even small wins lead to big transformations.

Every step you take with intention brings you closer to your dreams, making your time and energy count in the best way possible.

Set outcomes that inspire you, prioritize your efforts, and take time to reflect on your progress.

By focusing on purposeful actions instead of just staying busy, you'll create a life filled with achievements that matter.

Remember, time is precious—when you use it intentionally, it becomes the foundation for a future you're excited about.

You've got what it takes to make every moment count!

KEY #3

ASK BETTER QUESTIONS AND THRIVE FASTER

The questions you ask shape the opportunities you see and how you solve problems—start asking better questions, and you'll unlock new possibilities, deeper understanding, and smarter decisions.

Your life isn't meant to be lived on autopilot—it's a journey you get to shape. And one of the most powerful tools for steering your life in the direction you want?

Asking the right questions.

Great questions **spark fresh ideas, solve problems, uncover hidden obstacles, and open doors to exciting opportunities.**

They help you see challenges from new angles, break free from old patterns, and take control of your decisions with confidence.

Instead of accepting things as they are, thoughtful questions encourage you to dig deeper, explore new possibilities, and actively shape your future.

The quality of your life is directly tied to the quality of your questions.

Questions aren't just about getting answers—they're about creating possibilities.

If you're struggling with a challenge, a well-placed question can help you uncover what's really holding you back. **If you're feeling stuck, the right question will unlock solutions you hadn't considered.**

And if you're facing a big decision, asking the right questions will give you the clarity you need to move forward with confidence.

Think of questions as a compass—they help you navigate challenges, find clarity, and discover the best path forward.

Let's dive in and explore how asking better questions can transform your life!

THE POWER OF THE RIGHT QUESTION

Their favorite Common Grounds Café barista greeted them cheerfully as Sarah, Michael, and Emma gathered again at their familiar corner table.

It was a rainy afternoon, and the rhythmic tapping of raindrops against the window made atmosphere inside seem even more cozy.

As they chatted, the bell above the door jingled, and a tall figure stepped in, shaking the rain from his umbrella.

"Hey, there's Jack!" Sarah said, waving him over.

They hadn't seen Jack the last two times they'd gathered at the Common Grounds, and his absence had started to feel like a missing piece of their conversations.

Jack had a knack for offering thoughtful insights, often shifting their perspectives in ways they didn't expect, and his quick wit always brought a smile.

They had missed his steady presence. It just wasn't the same without him.

Jack smiled as he approached, his hair still damp from the rain. "Hey, guys," he said, pulling up a chair. "Looks like I came just in time."

Emma grinned. "We were just about to dive into another one of our life talks, so perfect timing."

She shot Michael a playful look. "Michael's got a dilemma, and I think you might have some good insights."

Michael let out a frustrated sigh. "Well, it's not exactly a new problem," he admitted. "It's about my career...again.

I've been struggling to figure out if I'm in the right place or if I should be making a big change. But every time I start thinking about it, I just get overwhelmed and end up asking myself, 'Why can't I figure this out?' and 'Why am I still stuck?' It's like I'm getting nowhere."

Jack leaned back in his chair, a thoughtful expression on his face. "I've been there before," he said. "But those questions aren't going to help you get unstuck. The questions you're asking are basically just reinforcing the idea that you're stuck."

Sarah nodded in agreement. "Exactly. When you ask questions like that, you're telling your brain to focus on why things are going wrong. You're not giving yourself any direction."

Michael's brow furrowed as he stirred his coffee. "So, what should I be asking then? I mean, I know I need to think differently, but I'm not even sure where to start."

Emma jumped in. "It's not just about asking any questions—it's about asking empowering questions," she said. "Instead of 'Why can't I figure this out?' what if you asked, 'What's one step I can take today to get closer to the clarity I need?' or 'What would I do if I knew I couldn't fail?' Those questions would push you toward action instead of just making you feel stuck."

Jack nodded. "Emma's right. It's the questions we ask that shape the way we think. When I was trying to get my first startup off the ground, I kept asking myself, 'What if this doesn't work?' It was a paralyzing thought, and I almost gave up. Then, a friend of mine who had two successful startups challenged me to change my question. He said, 'Instead of asking what if it doesn't work, ask what it would take to make it work.' That shift in focus changed everything for me."

Michael's eyes widened slightly as he considered his words. "So, you're saying that the questions I'm *not* asking could be the real problem?"

"Exactly," Jack replied. "Sometimes, the questions we avoid are the ones that would actually push us forward. You need to start asking yourself questions that might make you uncomfortable - questions that force you to really think. For example, 'Am I holding myself back because I'm afraid of what it will take to make a change?' or 'What specific skills do I need to develop to move into a new career?' Those kinds of questions demand real answers, not just excuses."

Sarah leaned in, her voice steady and confident. "And don't forget to challenge your assumptions. Just because you're struggling to make a decision doesn't mean there's something wrong with you. It could just be that you're asking the wrong questions. What if you asked, 'What assumptions am I making about this situation that might not be true?' That kind of question could open up new possibilities you haven't even considered."

Michael took a sip of his coffee, a small smile spreading across his face. "You guys are really making me realize how much I've been on autopilot. I thought I was thinking things through, but I've just been spinning my wheels with the same unempowering questions over and over."

Emma reached across the table and squeezed Michael's hand. "We all fall into that trap sometimes. The important thing is that you're becoming aware of it now. Think about it—if you asked better questions every day, imagine where you could be a year from now."

Jack raised his cup. "To asking better questions and getting better answers."

The others followed suit, lifting their coffee cups with a shared sense of purpose.

As they clinked their mugs together, Michael felt a shift in his mindset, as if the fog was beginning to clear. It wasn't that his problem had magically disappeared, but he felt encouraged now that he had a new tool to tackle it—one question at a time.

Michael left the café that day with a list of new questions scribbled in his notebook, ready to replace the old ones that had kept him stuck.

He knew that from now on, he would challenge himself to ask better questions, even if they made him uncomfortable. He realized that the path to a better life didn't start with having all the answers—it started with asking the right questions.

THE POWER OF QUESTIONS: SHAPING YOUR THINKING AND YOUR LIFE

Questions are the keys that unlock new possibilities and guide your thinking.

Every question you ask—whether big or small—steers your mind toward answers, insights, and actions.

The beauty of this process is that you're in control and by asking thoughtful, purposeful questions, you shape your outlook and create opportunities for growth and progress.

Your brain is an incredible problem-solving machine, always ready to spring into action when you give it a question to work on.

It's like having an inner brainstorming team that's always ready to help you solve problems or find new opportunities.

The beauty of this process is how creative and resourceful your brain can be.

It doesn't just give you the obvious answers—it sparks connections between things you might never have linked together.

For example, a challenge at work might remind you of a strategy you used in a completely different situation, and suddenly, you've got a solution you didn't expect.

Or, while reflecting on a personal goal, your brain might connect a conversation from months ago to a new opportunity that aligns perfectly with your vision.

These sparks of insight often come when you least expect them—during a walk, in the shower, or even while daydreaming. That's the magic of giving your brain a clear and empowering question to work on.

It's always processing, always searching for ways to move you forward, and the answers it provides can lead to breakthroughs that take you closer to your goals.

The more you nurture this process, the more your brain becomes a wellspring of creativity and problem-solving brilliance!

The most exciting part?

You're in charge of what questions it works on!

ASK THE RIGHT QUESTIONS TO GET THE RIGHT ANSWERS

Not all questions are equal and asking the right types of questions unlocks the door to progress and growth.

The way you form your questions shapes how you and others think, what is focused on, and ultimately, the answers you get.

The Power (and Pitfall) of "Why" Questions

Questions that begin with "why" can be incredibly valuable when used intentionally. They help you uncover root causes, gain clarity, and understand what's really going on beneath the surface.

For example, asking, "Why did this happen?" can help you identify patterns or mistakes that need addressing.

But here's where "why" questions need a little balance.

When used in moments of frustration, they can sometimes lead to a downward spiral of self-doubt or excuses.

Asking, "Why can't I succeed like others?" might lead your brain to unhelpful answers like, "Because I'm not good enough," or "Because things never go my way."

These types of answers don't solve anything—they just reinforce a victim mentality.

The key is to **reframe your questions to focus on solutions and possibilities.** Instead of asking, "Why is this so hard?" try, "What's one thing I can do to make this easier?" or "What resources can help me overcome this challenge?"

These types of questions encourage your brain to think creatively and identify positive, actionable steps.

USE EMPOWERING QUESTIONS TO SOLVE PROBLEMS AND BUILD MOMENTUM

Empowering questions focus on solutions and possibilities!

These high-quality questions are like fuel for your mind, guiding you toward constructive answers that help you move forward with confidence.

The secret lies in the words you choose—starting your questions with "how" and "what" make all the difference.

"How" and "What" Spark Solutions

When you ask "how" or "what" questions, you naturally shift your focus toward action and opportunity.

For example, asking, "How can I approach this differently?" or "What steps can I take to improve this situation?" invites your mind to explore creative solutions and new perspectives.

These types of questions help you take control and build momentum.

By making these high-quality questions a habit, you'll not only overcome challenges more effectively but also uncover exciting possibilities.

The right questions don't just solve problems—they open doors to growth and success.

UNLOCKING IDEAS—FOR YOURSELF AND OTHERS

Not only can the right questions help you discover ideas and solutions, but they can also **spark insights in others**—even people who may not have been eager to help at first.

When you ask thoughtful, open-ended questions, you encourage the people around you to **think differently, explore new perspectives, and uncover solutions they didn't realize they had.**

And sometimes, a well-placed question can even shift someone from being unwilling or uncertain to actively helping you.

Imagine you're working on a tough project, and a team member seems reluctant to get involved.

Instead of pushing them, you ask, "If you were tackling this, what's the first thing you'd try?" or "What would make this easier for you?"

Suddenly, they're thinking about solutions instead of reasons why they can't help. Without pressure, they start offering ideas—and before you know it, they're part of the solution.

Asking great questions isn't just about expanding your own thinking—it's about **activating the creativity and problem-solving skills of the people around you.** When you do, you'll uncover fresh ideas, gain unexpected insights, and open doors to opportunities you might never have found alone.

THE FORMULA FOR ASKING HIGH-QUALITY "WHAT" AND "HOW" QUESTIONS

The right question can change everything. It can shift your perspective, open up new possibilities, and lead you to creative solutions you wouldn't have considered otherwise.

But how do you ask questions that get real results?

To make this easy to use, I've created a simple formula you can use to make sure your questions are powerful, clear, and action-driven:

1. **Determine your outcome.**
   What do you want the question to accomplish? This gives your mind a clear direction. Be **as specific as necessary and as broad as possible** to allow for creative solutions.

2. **Add "What" or "How" to the beginning.**
   These words keep your questions **solution-focused** rather than leading you into frustration or excuses.

3. **Include a pronoun like "I," "you," "us," or "we"** to make it clear **who is responsible** for taking action.

Ask Better Questions And Thrive Faster

When you follow this formula, you create questions that lead to **insightful answers and real progress.**

Examples of High-Quality Questions Using This Formula

- Outcome: Find a way to be more productive at work.
  Question: *How can I work more efficiently and get the most important things done first?*

- Outcome: Improve communication within a team.
  Question: *What can we do to communicate more clearly and avoid misunderstandings?*

- Outcome: Overcome a financial challenge.
  Question: *How can I create a plan to get out of debt and build financial security?*

- Outcome: Solve a difficult problem.
  Question: *What options do we have to resolve this in a way that benefits everyone involved?*

- Outcome: Strengthen a relationship.
  Question: *How can I show appreciation and strengthen my connection with the people I care about?*

Why This Works

When you structure your questions this way, you **tell your brain to focus on solutions instead of problems.** Instead of getting stuck in frustration (like "Why is this happening to me?"), you start looking for actions that will move you forward.

So next time you're facing a challenge, pause and apply this formula. Ask yourself:

Am I asking a question that leads to real solutions?

When you do, you'll be surprised and delighted with the powerful insights you unlock!

THE POWER OF THE QUESTIONS YOU HAVEN'T ASKED

It's not just the questions you ask that shape your life—it's also the ones waiting to be asked.

These unspoken questions often hold the potential for breakthroughs, offering the clarity and insight you need to grow and thrive.

Sometimes, the most powerful questions are the ones that nudge you out of your comfort zone or invite you to reflect deeply.

The questions you've been holding back might just be the ones that lead to the growth and progress you're looking for.

So, what questions can you ask yourself today to spark new possibilities and take that next big step forward?

Create some high quality questions and let the answers guide you toward your best life!

ARE YOU ASKING GOOD QUESTIONS?

Asking high quality questions is a simple yet powerful way to shift your mindset and uncover new possibilities.

But how do you know if the questions you're asking are truly helping you grow and move forward?

These seven questions will help you evaluate whether you're on the right track, guiding you to reframe your thinking and focus on solutions, creativity, and progress. Let's dive in!

1. **Does this question focus on solutions rather than problems?**
   Example: Instead of asking, "Why did this go wrong?" try, "What can I do to fix it and move forward?"

2. **Does this question encourage action and progress?**
   Example: Swap "Why am I stuck?" with "How can I take the next small step toward my goal?"

3. **Am I framing this question in a way that builds confidence?**
   Example: Replace "Why do I always struggle with this?" with "What strengths can I use to tackle this challenge?"

4. **Is this question helping me uncover opportunities?**
   Example: Change "Why do I have bad luck?" to "What opportunities am I not seeing yet?"

5. **Does this question invite reflection and learning?**
   Example: Instead of "Why do I keep making mistakes?" ask, "What can I learn from this experience to improve next time?"

6. **Am I opening myself to creative solutions?**
   Example: Replace "Why is this so hard?" with "What if I approached this in a different way?"

7. **Does this question shift my focus toward what I can control?**
   Example: Instead of "Why isn't anyone helping me?" ask, "What steps can I take on my own to move closer to my goal?"

By reflecting on these questions, you'll ensure that the ones you ask are empowering, actionable, and aligned with your growth and success.

Let your questions guide you to new possibilities and meaningful progress!

them today to unlock new opportunities and create momentum in your life!

THE QUESTIONS YOU ASK SHAPE YOUR LIFE: QUESTIONS TO HELP YOU THRIVE FASTER

The right questions can change everything. They help you break through obstacles, uncover new opportunities, and take control of your growth.

But how often do you stop and think about the questions **you** are asking—both to yourself and to others?

Take a few moments to reflect—because the **quality of your life is directly tied to the quality of your questions.**

1. **What's a question I frequently ask myself—and is it empowering or limiting?**
   Does this question help me move forward, or does it focus on problems instead of solutions?

2. **When faced with a challenge, do I ask "Why is this happening to me?" or "How can I solve this?"**
   How can I reframe my questions to focus on action and possibility instead of frustration?

3. **What's one area of my life where asking better questions could lead to new insights or breakthroughs?**
   Where am I stuck, and what's a better question I can start asking to create progress?

4. **Do I use questions to help others think more deeply and uncover their own solutions?**
   How can I ask better questions in conversations to inspire new ideas and opportunities?

5. **If I could ask one question every morning to set the tone for a great day, what would it be?**
   What question can I start my day with that will keep me focused, motivated, and in the right mindset?

THE BOTTOM LINE

If you're ready to elevate your life and achieve extraordinary results, start by asking better questions.

High quality, empowering questions open the door to deeper insights, fresh perspectives, and exciting possibilities.

They challenge you to think differently, explore new ideas, and unlock your full potential.

When you ask thoughtful, solution-oriented questions, you'll uncover better answers, make more confident decisions, and see greater progress.

Life isn't something to passively accept—it's something to actively shape.

So, embrace the power of great questions, and start create the life you truly want!

KEY #4

FIND THE SWEET SPOT BETWEEN PASSION, STRENGTHS & PRACTICALITY

The advice to *"follow your passion and do what you love"* is inspiring—it sparks excitement, fuels dreams, and makes

---

> Thriving isn't just about chasing passion—it's about balancing what you love, what you're naturally good at, and what actually works in the real world.

---

success feel limitless.

But **passion alone isn't enough to create a fulfilling, sustainable life.**

True success comes from aligning what excites you with what you're naturally good at and applying both in a practical way.

Pursuing your passion can be exhilarating, but it also requires dedication, patience, and effort. Even the things we love doing come with challenges, hard work, and sometimes tedious tasks.

Find the Sweet Spot Between Passion, Strengths & Practicality

But when you build on your strengths, progress is easier, confidence grows, and success becomes more natural.

At the same time, life doesn't always hand you opportunities that perfectly align with your passion.

Sometimes, responsibilities or unexpected experiences may not seem exciting at first, but they can teach invaluable skills, open new doors, and set the foundation for long-term success.

When you balance passion, strengths, and practicality, you create **a life that's not only exciting but also sustainable and deeply fulfilling.**

You stay focused on your goals while remaining adaptable to life's twists and turns.

Let's explore how to harmonize what lights you up with what moves you forward—so you can build a life that's both inspiring and grounded.

THE PASSION BIND

It was a cool autumn evening, and the Common Grounds Café was filled with the rich aroma of freshly brewed coffee and the chatter of regulars who had come to escape the crisp air outside.

Sarah, Michael, Emma, and Jack had snagged their usual corner table, where the warm light from the window cast a golden glow on their faces. The four friends were back together again for their regular meet up to catch up on life, share ideas, and, as always, discuss your latest struggles.

Tonight, there was a heaviness in the air; things didn't feel quite right.

Sarah and Jack seemed unusually quiet, and it wasn't long before Emma, always perceptive, picked up on it.

"So, what's going on?" Emma asked, glancing between Sarah and Jack. "You two have been in your own worlds since we sat down."

Jack let out a frustrated sigh. "Well, since you asked…" He hesitated before continuing. "It's just—I'm starting to wonder if this whole 'follow your passion' thing is a trap."

Michael raised an eyebrow. "What do you mean?"

Jack shifted uncomfortably in his seat. "You know how I've been pouring everything into my startup, right? I'm passionate about it—I mean, I love the idea of building something from the ground up. But lately, it's like… I'm not even enjoying it anymore. I'm constantly stressed out about finances, working late nights, and putting out fires. I feel like I'm always running on empty. The whole point was to do what I love, but I'm starting to think it's just making my life miserable."

Emma tilted her head, her voice soft. "Do you still feel passionate about the actual work, or is the stress just overshadowing everything?"

Jack shook his head. "I don't know. I used to love coding and developing new features, but now, it's just a small part of what I actually do. Most of my time goes to dealing with investors, managing employees, and handling all the business stuff I don't really enjoy. I feel like I'm chasing this dream, but it's taking me further away from the life I want."

Michael nodded thoughtfully. "That's tough, Jack. I think a lot of people are in that place. They're told to follow their passion, but they don't realize that success still requires doing the hard, boring, or uncomfortable stuff. Passion can only take you so far."

Sarah, who had been listening intently, finally spoke up. "I get what you're saying, Jack. I'm struggling too, but for a different reason. You at least have a clear passion you're working on. I've been sitting around trying to figure out what mine even is. I keep thinking that if I can just find my 'one true passion,' everything will fall into place, and I'll finally have direction. But... I still don't know what it is."

Emma leaned in, her tone encouraging but firm. "Sarah, I think you're putting way too much pressure on yourself to find some magical passion that's going to solve everything. It's okay not to have it all figured out. Sometimes you just need to start doing things, even if they're not your dream job. At least that way, you have a chance of finding your passion while you're doing other things."

Sarah sighed. "But isn't that settling? I don't want to waste time doing things I don't enjoy. I thought I was supposed to find what I love and make it my life."

Jack chimed in. "That's exactly what I thought too, Sarah. But now I'm realizing that sometimes you have to do the things you don't love to get to the things you *do* love. I mean, sure, I'm passionate about the startup, but the reality is, running a business isn't always fun. If I had known how much of it would be managing spreadsheets and dealing with clients, I'm not sure I would've jumped in so quickly."

Michael, who had been listening quietly, finally spoke. "I think the problem is that we've been taught to think of passion as the only thing that matters. But real success, and even happiness, comes from being willing to do what's necessary—even if it's not fun or exciting—because it gets you closer to the life you want. It's not always about doing what you love; sometimes it's about loving what you do *because* you know it's taking you somewhere worthwhile."

Emma nodded in agreement. "Exactly. The truth is, if you're going to chase any big goal, there are going to be parts you don't enjoy. That doesn't mean you're on the wrong path—it just means you need to accept that passion isn't enough by itself. It needs to be combined with purpose and, honestly, a lot of hard work."

Sarah glanced at Jack. "So, what are you going to do, Jack? Are you thinking of giving up on the startup?"

Jack paused, then shook his head. "No, I'm not giving up. But I do need to change my mindset. I need to stop expecting everything to be fun or enjoyable all the time. If I focus more on why I'm doing this—building something meaningful, creating value for myself and my family—then maybe I can push through the parts I don't like and find my way back to the parts I do."

Sarah looked down at her coffee, deep in thought. "I guess I need to stop waiting around for the perfect passion to fall into my lap. Maybe I just need to start doing things, even if they're not 'the one.' At least then, I'd be moving forward instead of just sitting here, hoping for some kind of magic spark."

Michael smiled. "You've got it, Sarah. Action leads to clarity, not the other way around. Start with what you can do, not just what you want to do."

Emma raised her mug, her eyes bright. "To taking action—even when it's not our passion. Because sometimes the path we need to take isn't the one we love."

The others followed suit, raising their cups in a shared sense of determination.

As they clinked their mugs together, Sarah and Jack felt a small but significant shift in their outlook. They didn't have all the answers yet, but they were beginning to see that the path to a meaningful life wasn't paved only with passion—it was built through purposeful action, grit, and a willingness to embrace the hard and sometimes unpleasant work that would be needed.

As the rain drizzled outside, the conversation continued, and the café felt warmer than before.

They knew that following their passion wasn't the problem; the real challenge was learning to do the necessary things that might not be fun but were essential to making their dreams a reality.

And that realization was a step in the right direction.

THE REALITY OF SUCCESS: EMBRACING THE JOURNEY

It's inspiring to think that following your passion will naturally lead to success, and while passion is an important starting point, **thriving is about more than just doing what you love.**

True achievement often comes from balancing your passion with the determination to take on the tasks that move you closer to your goals, even if they aren't fun or exciting.

Think about athletes who love their sport.

Their passion fuels them, but their success is built on a foundation of dedication—hours of training, disciplined routines, and drills that might not spark joy but are essential to their growth.

Those seemingly mundane moments are the building blocks of their greatness.

The same is true in business, relationships, or personal growth.

Find the Sweet Spot Between Passion, Strengths & Practicality

Success often requires stepping outside your comfort zone, embracing challenges, and doing the work that lays the groundwork for big wins.

By pairing your passion with a willingness to tackle what's necessary, you create a path to a fulfilling and well-rounded life.

Every step, no matter how small or tedious, brings you closer to your dreams.

WHEN LIFE ASKS FOR MORE

Following your passion is exciting and fulfilling, and when your passion reflects a deep value, it becomes a powerful force in your life.

But **thriving goes beyond simply pursuing what excites you**—it's about balancing your passion with the responsibilities and opportunities life brings.

Think about the many roles you play—parent, partner, friend, or community member.

These roles often involve doing things that don't directly align with your passion but still reflect your core values and contribute to your overall well being.

Supporting a loved one, taking on a job to provide for your family, or volunteering for a cause you care about may not always feel thrilling, but they contribute to a thriving life filled with purpose and connection.

Even when your passion is deeply tied to your values, thriving requires flexibility.

You might need to embrace tasks or challenges that indirectly support your passion, like developing new skills, managing logistics, or stepping into responsibilities that are difficult and uncomfortable.

These moments don't detract from your passion—they enhance it by creating a strong foundation for long-term success.

Ask yourself: "How can I align my passion with my strengths and real-world opportunities and necessities to create lasting success?"

That's the balance that makes long-term fulfillment possible.

FINDING THE RIGHT BALANCE

It's natural to have some doubts and questions when it comes to balancing passion, strengths, and practicality because it might mean **compromising your passion or settling for something less fulfilling.**

Maybe you're thinking, "But what if my passion doesn't align with my strengths?" or "What if being practical means giving up on what I love?"

These are valid concerns, and you're not alone in wondering about them so let's explore some common concerns and find out how to approach them with a fresh perspective.

I don't think my strengths align with my passion. What if I love something but I'm not naturally good at it?
Passion and strengths don't always align so it's possible

that you may not be able to make your passion your full time job.

For example, I love to play golf, but I've never been particularly athletic and coordinated so while I enjoy golf, I can't expect to be a golf pro. My strengths simply don't align with my passion.

The key is to identify areas where your natural abilities give you an edge and then look for ways to integrate your passion.

For me, this was using my strength as the owner of a software company to go into business with Arnold Palmer – one of the greatest golfers of all time. While it didn't help me to play better, it got me around parts of the sport that would have never experienced otherwise.

Sometimes, the best opportunities come from using your strengths to support what you love rather than making passion the only focus.

Focusing on strengths feels limiting—what if I want to explore new things?
Balancing strengths with passion doesn't mean you can't grow or explore new interests.

In fact, leveraging what you're already good at gives you a foundation for expanding into new areas.

You can always build new skills, pivot, or evolve, but understanding and using your natural strengths makes that journey smoother. Instead of seeing strengths as a limitation, think of them as a launchpad for bigger opportunities.

Being practical sounds like giving up on my dreams.
Being practical isn't about abandoning your dreams—it's about making them achievable.

Passion alone doesn't guarantee success, but when you pair it with smart, strategic action, you create a real path forward.

Taking practical steps toward your goals doesn't mean settling—it means making long-term success more likely.

Your dream doesn't disappear just because you approach it with wisdom.

I don't want to get stuck doing something just because I'm good at it.
That's completely understandable!

Fortunately, the good news is that just because you have a strength in something doesn't mean it has to define your entire path.

The goal is to <u>use your strengths as a tool, not a cage.</u>

If you're good at something but don't enjoy it, look for ways to apply that skill in a different way—perhaps in a new industry, a side project, or as a stepping stone toward something that excites you more.

Strengths are meant to support your passion, not replace it.

The Takeaway

Balancing passion, strengths, and practicality **isn't about choosing one over the other—it's about making them work together.**

Find the Sweet Spot Between Passion, Strengths & Practicality

When you lean into what excites you, use what you're naturally good at, and take smart steps forward, you create a path that's both fulfilling and sustainable.

Instead of asking, *"Do I follow my passion or do what makes sense?"* try asking, *"How can I use my strengths to fuel my passion in a way that works in the real world?"*

That's where true thriving happens.

ALIGNING PASSION WITH PURPOSE: OPENING THE DOOR TO TRUE FULFILLMENT

Following your passion is exciting and energizing, but the path to what you truly want is often richer and more dynamic than just doing what you love.

By staying open to opportunities that might not seem thrilling at first, you can discover rewarding paths that lead to greater growth and fulfillment.

For example, imagine someone who loves cooking and dreams of opening a restaurant. Their passion for creating meals for everyone to enjoy is a wonderful foundation, but running a restaurant involves much more—it's about managing a team, working with suppliers, and navigating daily business operations.

Over time, they may even find unexpected joy in the business side of things, deepening their overall fulfillment. But even if those tasks don't excite them, they're essential to supporting the business that supports their passion.

And **sometimes, life calls us to step outside of our passion entirely to focus on what's most important**—whether it's supporting a loved one, meeting a family responsibility, or taking on a challenge that helps us grow in new ways.

These moments may not always align perfectly with our passion but are part of a well balanced, thriving life.

THE VALUE OF BALANCING PASSION WITH GROWTH

Pursuing what you love is exciting and energizing, but there's even more to gain when you expand your horizons.

By exploring new opportunities and embracing challenges beyond your passion, you open the door to valuable experiences, skills, and connections that can enhance your journey in ways you never imagined.

These moments of growth often lead to breakthroughs that passion alone might not achieve.

Stepping outside your comfort zone and trying something new can be transformative.

While it may not always feel easy, these experiences help you grow stronger, more adaptable, and better equipped to handle life's opportunities. Often, the things that feel like a stretch are the very things that propel you to the next level.

Balancing passion with practicality and personal growth ensures that you're not only pursuing what excites you but also building a foundation for long-term success and fulfillment.

It's this combination that allows you to thrive in every area of life!

Find the Sweet Spot Between Passion, Strengths & Practicality

STRENGTHS OR WEAKNESSES—WHERE SHOULD YOU FOCUS?

I get this question all the time and you've probably heard both sides of this debate:

"Fix your weaknesses—they're what's holding you back!"

"No, double down on your strengths—that's where the magic is!"

So... which is it?

Well, like most things in life, the answer isn't black and white. It depends. But here's the good news: you don't have to choose one or the other.

The smartest path forward?

Use your strengths as fuel—and handle your weaknesses wisely.

Emma's Strength Was Holding Her Back— Until She Saw the Bigger Picture

Emma was a natural on camera.

Her voice was warm and clear, and she had that rare gift of making people feel like she was speaking directly to them—even through a screen.

Her strength? Communication.

It was easy for her and she loved it, and it showed.

So when she launched her online coaching business, she assumed success would follow.

But behind the scenes, things weren't quite working.

She was missing deadlines. Losing track of client notes. Sometimes, she forgot to send follow-up emails entirely.

It wasn't a talent issue—it was a system issue.

Organizing things was painful for her, so Emma avoided structure like the plague. Planning, tracking, organizing—it all felt stiff and unnatural.

And so, she just didn't do it.

Eventually, she realized her brilliance on camera wasn't enough and that her lack of organization was undercutting everything she worked for.

Instead of trying to turn herself into a planner-type, she did two smart things:

1. She got a simple system she could actually stick with.
2. She hired someone who *loved* spreadsheets.

Now, Emma still leads with her strength—but she's no longer held back by the weakness.

That's the magic of using your strengths wisely—without letting your weaknesses sabotage your success.

Here's how you can do the same:

Smart Strategies for Managing Strengths and Weaknesses

- *Start with your goals.* What are you trying to accomplish? What strengths will help you get there? Are there any weak spots that might block your progress? You don't need to be perfect—but you do need to be strategic.

- *Ignore the irrelevant.* If your goal is to launch a successful podcast, who cares if you can't run a 5K or bake a soufflé? Not all weaknesses matter. Focus only on the ones that get in your way.

- *Watch for "everywhere" weaknesses.* Some challenges—like procrastination, indecisiveness, or not following through—show up *everywhere*. These are worth your attention because they limit your potential in all areas of your life.

- *Leverage other people's strengths.* You don't have to be able to do everything yourself. One of the smartest moves? Build a team where others are strong where you're not. That's the power of partnership.

- *Be honest about diminishing returns.* If you're already great at something, putting more time into it probably won't move the needle very much. Sometimes your next level isn't about getting better—it's about removing what's holding you back.

- *Don't let your ego drive the bus.* It feels good to do what we're already good at. But growth often means spending time in the uncomfortable zone. Keep your eyes on the outcome—not just what feels safe.

You were born with unique strengths. They're not random. They're part of your gift to the world.

But thriving isn't just about playing to your strengths. It's about being wise. Being intentional.

And having the courage to shore up the cracks that could keep your brilliance from shining through.

Make the call:

What strengths will you double down on?

What weaknesses are worth your time?

A BALANCED APPROACH: PASSION, STRENGTHS, AND DISCIPLINE

Passion is a wonderful force—it's the spark that lights you up and fills your life with excitement and energy.

It inspires big dreams and fuels your enthusiasm for the things that matter most to you. But to truly thrive, **passion shines brightest when paired with your strengths and discipline**, creating a balance that helps you stay focused and move steadily toward your goals.

While passion gives you energy and drive, it's your purpose and long-term perspective that guide you.

Necessity helps you connect your passion to a bigger picture, giving meaning to the steps you take, even the ones that don't feel exciting in the moment. Whether it's learning a new skill, managing your finances, or tackling a tough conversation, these practical steps are the building blocks of your success.

Passion reminds you why these efforts matter and keeps you motivated through the process.

Taking a long-term view makes all the difference. When you ask yourself, "What will this effort lead to in a year or

Find the Sweet Spot Between Passion, Strengths & Practicality

five years?" you shift your focus from the temporary challenge to the lasting rewards ahead.

For more about taking a long-term view *see Future Proof Your Decisions* on page 47.

This longer term view helps you embrace each step as part of the journey, empowering you to move forward with clarity and confidence.

By combining the excitement of passion, the clarity of purpose, and the steadiness of discipline, you create a strong foundation for long-term success and fulfillment.

It's not just about starting strong—it's about staying the course and enjoying the incredible rewards that come from aligning your passion and strengths with purposeful action.

ARE YOU ONLY FOLLOWING YOUR PASSION?

Following your passion is exciting but thriving means finding the right balance between doing what you love and focusing on what truly matters.

Here are some questions to help you reflect and make sure that while you pursue your passion, you're also taking care of the important steps that support your growth, relationships, and long-term success.

1. **Does this align with my long-term goals?**
   Example: "I love designing logos, but is this helping me build my dream of running a full-service branding agency?"

2. **Am I prioritizing tasks that support my overall growth?**
   Example: "I enjoy writing blog posts, but am I also focusing on building relationships with potential clients?"

3. **Is there a practical step I'm avoiding because it doesn't feel exciting?**
   Example: "I love crafting my product, but am I putting off setting up my budget or managing inventory?"

4. **Am I neglecting important relationships or responsibilities?**
   Example: "I'm passionate about my art, but am I making enough time to connect with my family or friends?"

5. **Is my passion leading to financial stability or strain?**
   Example: "I love teaching yoga, but am I also taking steps to ensure my income supports my long-term needs?"

6. **What skills or knowledge could I develop to support my passion more effectively?**
   Example: "I'm passionate about photography, but could learning business or marketing help me grow my career?"

7. **Am I staying open to opportunities that may not initially excite me?**
   Example: "I love my current project, but could saying yes to this networking event open doors to new possibilities?"

By asking yourself these questions, you'll make sure that your passion is balanced with the steps and priorities that support a fulfilling, well-rounded life.

Find the Sweet Spot Between Passion, Strengths & Practicality

QUESTIONS TO HELP YOU FIND YOUR SWEET SPOT

We all want to do what we love, but **thriving isn't just about passion—it's about aligning what excites you with what you're naturally good at and what works in the real world.**

When you find that balance, progress is easier, opportunities open up, and success becomes sustainable.

These five reflection questions will help you step back and evaluate where you are now, where you want to go, and how to bridge the gap in a way that feels both exciting and achievable.

Take a few moments to reflect—because when you find your sweet spot, you're no longer just chasing success, you're building it.

1. **What's one thing I'm passionate about, and how do my natural strengths support it?**
   Are there skills I already have that can help me turn my passion into something meaningful?

2. **Where have I been relying on passion alone without considering my strengths or practical steps?**
   Am I expecting excitement to carry me forward without developing the necessary skills or strategies?

3. **How can I use my strengths in a way that excites me and creates real opportunities?**
   Instead of forcing a path that isn't working, how can I

apply what I'm great at in a way that aligns with what I love?

4. **What practical steps can I take today to bring my passion and strengths together?**
   Am I actively creating a bridge between what I love and what's possible, or just hoping things will fall into place?

5. **What unexpected opportunities have helped me grow—even when they didn't seem connected to my passion at first?**
   How can I stay open to new paths that strengthen my skills and set me up for success?

THE BOTTOM LINE

If you want to create a life that's truly thriving, **remember that success isn't always effortless or exciting—and that's okay.**

Some of the most rewarding achievements come from doing the necessary work, even when it's not the most thrilling part of the journey.

By embracing challenges and staying committed, you set yourself up for real growth and lasting success.

Building a thriving life isn't just about doing what you love; it's about using your strengths, staying adaptable, and being willing to push through discomfort.

The best opportunities often come from persistence, from showing up even when it's hard, and from learning to navigate the less glamorous steps along the way.

Find the Sweet Spot Between Passion, Strengths & Practicality

Passion can light the spark, but it's perseverance, focus, and action that will carry you toward lasting success.

You've got what it takes—stay the course, trust the process, and the results will be worth it!

KEY #5

SEE CLEARLY AND DREAM BOLDLY

Big dreams drive success, but real progress comes from balancing ambition with a clear understanding of reality—so you can take practical steps toward making your vision happen.

Dreaming big is one of the most exciting parts of life—it allows you to **see beyond your current reality and imagine what's truly possible.**

Your dreams fuel your ambition, push you past self-doubt, and inspire you to aim higher. They give you the energy to overcome challenges and focus on what could be.

But the real magic happens when you **pair your vision with a clear understanding of reality.**

Think of it like building a skyscraper: your dream is the blueprint that inspires you, and reality is the foundation that makes it strong. One without the other won't stand the test of time.

See Clearly And Dream Boldly

When you embrace the world as it is, you gain the clarity to take practical, strategic steps toward what you want—turning dreams into something real.

Success isn't about choosing between being a dreamer and being practical. It's about knowing when to adapt to reality instead of pushing ahead blindly.

By seeing things clearly and making informed decisions, you set yourself up for real, lasting progress.

So, dream big—and take smart steps forward.

When you combine bold vision with thoughtful action, your dreams don't just stay in your imagination—they become your reality.

THE REALITY CHECK

The Common Grounds Café buzzed with conversation as the four friends gathered around their usual corner table.

The scent of freshly brewed coffee filled the air, but today, the atmosphere between them was heavier than usual. Michael kept glancing out the window, where the sun was setting behind the city skyline, casting long shadows over the snow covered streets.

"I just don't know what to do," Michael finally said, breaking the silence.

He ran a hand through his hair and sighed. "I'm struggling to figure out whether I should take this job offer. It's a big step up, but something doesn't feel right. I keep thinking, 'Am I just scared of change, or is there something really off here?' I can't tell if the doubts are in my head or if they're warning signs I should be paying attention to."

Emma leaned in, her expression sympathetic as always. "I get it, Michael. It's hard to know if what you're feeling is reality or just your own fears talking. It's easy to get caught up in your thoughts and lose track of what's actually true."

Sarah nodded in agreement. "You're definitely not alone, Michael. I went through something similar when I decided to leave my last job. I kept telling myself everything would get better if I just waited it out. But deep down, I knew the culture was toxic, and it wasn't going to change no matter how much I wished it would. I was angry when I realized the reality wasn't the way I wanted it to be."

Michael glanced over at her, curiosity flickering in his eyes. "How did you come to terms with that? I mean, how did you reconcile what you wanted with what was actually happening?"

Sarah leaned back in her chair, folding her arms as she reflected. "At first, I was mad—at my boss, at the company, even at myself. I felt like I had been living in denial, holding onto this fantasy that things would improve if I just kept my head down and worked harder. But when I finally admitted to myself that things weren't going to change, I realized I had a choice. I could either stay stuck and keep wishing things were different, or I could face the reality, even if it was uncomfortable, and take action."

She took a sip of her coffee before continuing. "Once I accepted that reality wasn't going to magically align with how I wanted it to be, I started looking at what I *could* control. I focused on updating my skills, building my network, and finding a workplace where the culture was actually healthy. It wasn't about giving up on what I wanted—it was about finding a different path to get there."

Jack, who had been listening quietly, chimed in. "I think that's where a lot of people get stuck—myself included. We cling to the way we think things *should* be and end up ignoring the signs that they aren't. I did that with my first business idea. I kept telling myself it was just a matter of time before things took off because I believed so strongly in it. But the reality was that there wasn't a market for the product. I had to admit that to myself, and it felt like a punch in the gut. But once I accepted the truth, I could shift my focus to something that had proven demand."

Michael frowned thoughtfully. "So, you're saying I need to figure out if my concerns are based on something real, or if I'm just overthinking?"

"Exactly," Sarah said. "It's about getting clear on the facts. Look at the situation objectively—what's actually happening and what's just your perception? If there are genuine red flags, you need to take them seriously. But if it's just fear or doubt clouding your judgment, then it's time to push through those feelings and take the leap."

Jack nodded in agreement. "And it helps to talk to people who can give you a different perspective. When I was stuck, I reached out to some advisors and even customers for their input. It gave me a reality check I desperately needed. Sometimes, other people can see things you're too close to recognize."

Emma smiled warmly. "You've got this, Michael. Don't get lost in the 'what if's.' Ground yourself in the facts, weigh the risks, and remember that reality doesn't have to be the way you wish it was for you to still make the best of it."

Michael took a deep breath, his shoulders relaxing slightly. "You're right. I've been caught up in trying to make sure this decision feels perfect, but maybe that's not realistic. I need to focus on what's real and then decide if it's a risk I'm willing to take."

Sarah raised her cup. "To facing reality, even when it's not what we want, and using it to create the life we can have."

The others followed suit, lifting their mugs in solidarity just like they always did after a meaningful conversation.

As they clinked their cups together, Michael felt a small but significant shift in his mindset. He knew that embracing reality, rather than fighting against it, would help him make a better decision. It was time to step out of the fog of uncertainty and see things as they truly were.

As the four friends continued to chat, the café lights flickered on, casting their usual warm glow over the table.

Michael knew the path ahead might not be easy, but at least now, he could approach it with clarity.

He was ready to confront the facts and make his choice—not based on how he wished things were, but on the reality of what they really were.

REALITY AND PERCEPTION: BUILDING A CLEARER VIEW

Have you ever had a moment when you thought you had everything figured out, only to discover there was more to the story?

I think we all have!

And when it happens, it's a powerful moment because perception doesn't always match reality and when you recognize it, this awareness isn't a setback; it's an opportunity.

The more clearly you see things, the better decisions you can make, and the more effectively you can move forward.

We all experience the world through our own unique mental filters, shaped by our beliefs, experiences, and expectations.

To enable us to function in the modern world, our brains are wired to simplify the flood of information we take in every day, using shortcuts like generalizations, deletions, and distortions to make sense of it all.

This is a brilliant tool for navigating life—but it's also a reminder to pause and double-check the "maps" we're using to guide our choices.

Sometimes, we hold on to how we *wish* things were because it feels comfortable or hopeful. Other times, we simply don't have all the information we need, and our minds fill in the gaps.

When we recognize this, we **get the opportunity to explore a clearer picture of reality**—one that allows us to **align our actions with what's truly happening.**

Seeing things as they are, rather than as we wish them to be, isn't about letting go of hope or optimism. It's about grounding ourselves in clarity and truth so we can **make better decisions, take effective action, and thrive.**

With a clear understanding of both reality and perception, we can navigate life with confidence and purpose, knowing we're moving forward on solid ground.

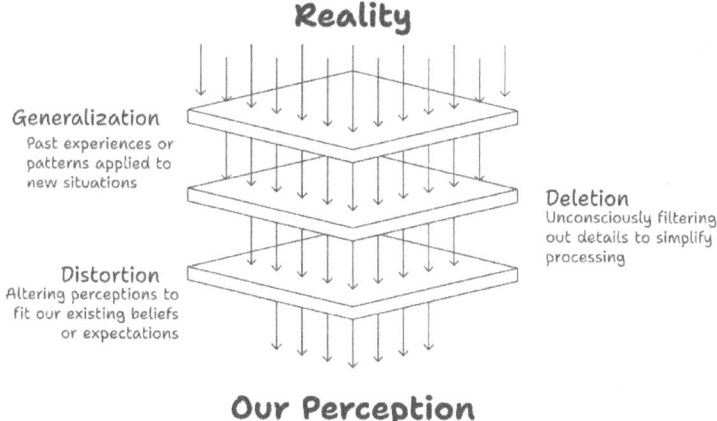

EMBRACING REALITY: THE KEY TO CLARITY AND PROGRESS

Interacting with the world as it truly is feels empowering and liberating.

When you face reality head-on (even if it's unpleasant), you open the door to **new opportunities, better decisions, and meaningful progress.**

It's not about letting go of your dreams or optimism—it's about using reality as your foundation to build something extraordinary.

Here's what happens when you embrace reality:

- **Uncover Solutions:** Acknowledging challenges allows you to address them proactively. Instead of avoiding problems, you gain the clarity and confidence to solve them.
  Example: Identifying why a product isn't selling helps you adjust pricing, improve marketing, or better meet customer needs.

- **Make Smarter Decisions:** When you recognize obstacles and risks, you can make informed choices that move you closer to your goals.
  Example: Instead of hoping for things to improve on their own, you take actionable steps to turn the tide in your favor.

- **Create Real Progress:** Balancing optimism with practical action ensures you're not just wishing for a better outcome but actively creating one.
  Example: If something isn't working, seeing the truth helps you pivot and try new strategies that lead to success.

The good news?

Reality isn't something to fear—it's your strongest ally.

When you see things as they are, you gain the power to adapt, improve, and grow. Facing reality with courage and curiosity gives you the tools to create the future you truly desire.

With a clear perspective, you can turn challenges into opportunities and dreams into achievable goals. Reality is your starting point, and the possibilities are endless!

POSITIVE THINKING GROUNDED IN REALITY: A WINNING COMBINATION

Positive thinking is a powerful mindset that fuels hope, resilience, and confidence.

It's about more than simply "seeing the glass as half-full"— it's about choosing to focus on possibilities, staying motivated through challenges, and believing in your ability to overcome setbacks.

When used wisely, a positive mindset fuels hope, resilience, and confidence—helping you turn obstacles into opportunities and keep moving forward with purpose.

What makes positive thinking truly transformative is balancing it with a clear understanding of reality.

It's not about ignoring problems or pretending everything is perfect.

Instead, it's about acknowledging difficulties and fixing them or viewing them as stepping stones for growth and improvement. This balance allows you to stay solution-focused and optimistic, even when life throws you a curveball.

Think of it as embracing reality with a mindset that says, "I've got this—I can make it work."

By facing facts honestly while maintaining hope and determination, you empower yourself to make thoughtful decisions and take meaningful action. Positive thinking becomes your tool for turning dreams into plans and challenges into triumphs.

With this balanced approach, you don't just imagine a better future—you actively create it.

It's about blending hope with practicality to ensure that you thrive, no matter the situation. Together, positive thinking and a realistic perspective create a foundation for success, resilience, and growth.

When you balance optimism with a realistic perspective, you empower yourself to make progress with confidence.

It's not about wishing things were different—it's about believing in your ability to make them better and taking the steps to create the outcomes you desire. With this mindset, you can achieve extraordinary things!

WHEN TO DREAM BIG AND WHEN TO STAY GROUNDED

Dreams are the spark that fuels progress and inspires you to reach for something greater. They give you hope, direction, and the courage to push beyond what seems possible.

When paired with a clear understanding of reality, dreams become the motivation for transforming your aspirations into achievements.

Let your dreams guide you when you're setting bold goals, seeking inspiration, or finding the courage to tackle something new.

Dreams help you see the bigger picture and focus on what's possible rather than being held back by limitations. They're **the power source that propels you forward**, showing you a life that's more meaningful and fulfilling.

At the same time, grounding yourself in reality is what makes those dreams achievable. While **dreams provide the vision, reality ensures your efforts are focused, effective, and result in lasting success.**

Reality matters when you're making plans, because it makes sure you assess your resources, challenges, and next steps with clarity. It's equally important when you're evaluating progress, because it allows you to **see what's working, what needs adjustment, and where to go next.**

Think of it this way: your dreams show you your destination, while reality is the map that reveals the obstacles and path, guiding you and keeping you on track.

Together, they create a powerful combination, ensuring you're both inspired and strategic.

When you feel stuck or unsure, ask yourself:

Am I dreaming big enough to stay inspired?

Am I grounded enough to understand the current challenges?

By balancing these two perspectives, you create a life where your dreams come to life and your reality becomes something you're proud of.

With this harmony, the possibilities are endless!

BE CAREFUL OF "SHOULD"

Making thoughtful, grounded decisions is critical to making meaningful progress in your life.

While it's natural to think about how things *should* be, success comes from embracing how things *are* and using that knowledge to your advantage.

A mindset focused on "should" might sound like:

- "People should be honest, so I don't need to double-check this agreement."

- "This business idea should take off because it's such a great concept."
- "I should get a promotion because I'm the best person here."

You might even be absolutely right that things *should* work a certain way, but if reality doesn't match up, the best thing you can do is **adjust your approach and take action based on what's actually happening.** That way, you're setting yourself up for success instead of frustration.

Thriving requires pairing optimism with a realistic perspective and the beauty of seeing the world as it truly is lies in the clarity and control it gives you.

By understanding the current situation, you can create strategies that work, anticipate challenges, and turn opportunities into meaningful outcomes.

By moving beyond how things "should" be and embracing how they *are,* you set yourself up for growth, resilience, and achievements that stand the test of time.

Success isn't about wishing—it's about taking thoughtful, informed action to create the future you want. And that's a path worth following!

EMBRACING REALITY: THE FIRST STEP TOWARD THRIVING

Reality can sometimes be challenging to face, but it's also an incredible opportunity for growth and transformation.

Accurately determining and acknowledging where you are—whether it's recognizing areas where your skills need improvement, taking an honest look at your finances, or reevaluating a relationship—is the first step toward creating meaningful change.

Rather than avoiding discomfort, **embracing reality allows you to take control of your journey.**

Understanding reality allows you to ask yourself thoughtful, honest questions and use the answers to guide your next steps. This kind of clarity helps you identify what's working, what needs adjustment, and where to focus your efforts.

Embracing reality doesn't mean giving up on your dreams—it means giving them a strong foundation. By addressing challenges head-on and taking purposeful action, you set yourself up for progress and success.

Every step you take, no matter how small, brings you closer to the life you truly want. And that's a journey worth celebrating!

ARE YOU ARE FACING REALITY?

Here are some questions you can use to help determine whether you're ignoring reality and interacting with the world the way you wish it was, rather than how it truly is:

1. **Do I avoid uncomfortable truths or facts because they don't fit with the way I want things to be?**
   For example, am I ignoring financial problems, relationship issues, or career setbacks because facing them feels overwhelming?

2. **Do I make decisions based on how I think things *should* work, rather than how they actually do?**

If you find yourself frustrated when things don't go as planned, it could be a sign that you're operating based on wishful thinking.

3. **Am I relying on hope alone to solve my problems, instead of taking practical steps to address the situation?**
Hope is important, but without action, it won't change anything.

4. **Am I basing my expectations on ideal outcomes instead of considering potential obstacles and setbacks?**
Have I failed to prepare for challenges because I assumed everything will go perfectly according to plan?

5. **Am I ignoring feedback or advice from others because it conflicts with what I want to believe?**
When I hear something that challenges my assumptions, do I dismiss it rather than taking it seriously?

6. **Do I avoid asking tough questions about my situation because I'm afraid of what the answers might reveal?**
If you shy away from self-reflection or honest evaluation, you may be trying to protect yourself from reality.

7. **Am I holding onto unrealistic goals or timelines, despite evidence suggesting that I need to adjust my approach?**
Sticking to a plan out of stubbornness, even when it's

clearly not working, can indicate a refusal to accept reality.

Use the answers to these questions to take a deeper look at whether you're aligning your actions with the world as it is or focusing on how you wish it would be.

HOW TO DETERMINE REALITY

It's not always easy to determine the difference between how we think things are and how they really are, so here are some steps you can take to determine reality vs. perception.

Define the Situation Clearly

Start by clearly stating what your situation is. Be specific about the challenge, problem, or decision you're facing.

Example: "I'm not getting any responses to my job applications."

List the Known Facts

Write down all the facts you know about the situation. Focus on information that can be objectively verified.

Example: "I have applied to 15 companies in the last month. I have not received any interview invitations."

Identify Assumptions and Beliefs

List any assumptions you are making about the situation, such as why you think things are happening the way they are.

Example: "I assume I'm not getting responses because companies aren't hiring right now."

Separate Facts from Assumptions

Compare your list of facts with your assumptions to identify what is based on evidence and what is based on perception.

Example: "While it's true that some companies aren't hiring, I don't have any evidence that this is the case for all the companies I've applied to."

Seek Input from Other Perspectives

Ask others for their insights on the situation. This could include experts, colleagues, friends, or anyone who has relevant knowledge or experience.

Be careful not to select only people who have your same problem and are only guessing about what is happening and what you should do.

Example: Talk to someone in HR or a hiring manager to understand what they're currently looking for in candidates.

Analyze Emotional Influences

Take a moment to check in with yourself—are your emotions shaping how you see the situation? Feelings like fear, frustration, or hope can sometimes color our perspective without us realizing it.

Example: "Am I feeling discouraged and assuming that no one wants to hire me, even though I haven't gotten any direct feedback yet?"

Your emotions are completely valid, and it's okay to feel them! But separating feelings from facts helps you see things more clearly and make decisions based on what's really happening—not just how it feels in the moment.

Look for Patterns Over Time

Review your past experiences and any data you can gather to identify trends.

Example: "Have I consistently had trouble finding a job, or is this a new issue that started recently? Are there specific industries where I'm more likely to get a response?"

Review Your Dreams

Are my current actions supported by evidence or just hope?

Example: Have I validated my ideas with research, data, or feedback, or am I relying solely on wishful thinking?

HOW TO ENGAGE WITH REALITY EFFECTIVELY

It's easy to get caught up in how we *wish* things were, but real progress comes from seeing the world as it *actually* is.

When you engage with reality effectively, you make smarter decisions, avoid unnecessary setbacks, and create real momentum toward your goals.

Here are five simple strategies to help you stay clear-headed and focused on what truly matters:

Get Clear on the Facts

Making decisions based on assumptions instead of facts can lead you down the wrong path. The more accurate information you have, the better choices you can make.

Try this: Ask yourself, "What are the actual facts of this situation, and what do I *wish* they were?" Separating reality from wishful thinking gives you a clearer perspective and helps you move forward wisely.

Example: If your business isn't growing as fast as you'd like, instead of assuming "It should be successful by now," look at the numbers, customer feedback, and market conditions to understand what's really happening.

Challenge Your Assumptions

Just because something *feels* true doesn't mean it *is* true. Challenging your assumptions helps you avoid blind spots and see opportunities you might have missed.

Try this: Ask yourself, "What am I assuming about this situation, and what would I do differently if I knew that assumption was false?"

Example: If you assume "Networking doesn't work for me" but haven't actually followed up with people consistently, challenge that belief and try a new approach before deciding it's not for you.

Embrace Discomfort as Part of Growth

Reality isn't always comfortable, but discomfort often signals a chance to grow and improve. The key is learning to face challenges instead of avoiding them.

Try this: Instead of resisting uncomfortable truths, ask yourself, "What actions can I take to improve this situation?" Let discomfort be a motivator, not a roadblock.

Example: If you're struggling in a new role at work, rather than thinking "I'm just not good at this," reframe it as "What skills can I develop to get better?"

See *Ask Better Questions* on page 89

Balance Optimism with Reality

Staying positive is powerful, but ignoring reality can set you up for disappointment. The most successful people are both positive and prepared.

Try this: Use the "expect the best, prepare for the worst" approach. Stay optimistic, but also consider potential obstacles and plan accordingly.

Example: If you're launching a new product, believing "It's going to be a huge success" is great—but having a backup plan for slow initial sales will keep you from being caught off guard.

EVALUATE YOUR DREAMS: TURNING VISION INTO REALITY

Dreaming big is essential—your dreams set the direction for where you want to go. But to make them a reality, they need to be supported by action, strategy, and real-world feedback.

Ask yourself: Are my current actions backed by evidence, or am I relying solely on hope?

Example: If you're starting a business, have you tested your idea with research, data, or feedback, or are you assuming "This *should* work because I believe in it"?

Regularly Check Your Progress

Sometimes, we get stuck in routines or keep pushing forward without realizing that something isn't working. Checking in with reality helps you adjust and improve.

Try this: Ask yourself, "Am I making the progress I expected, or do I need to adjust my approach?"

Example: If your fitness plan isn't delivering results, instead of thinking "This should be working," take an honest look at your habits and tweak them based on what's *actually* effective.

QUESTIONS TO STRENGTHEN YOUR VISION AND ACTION

Big dreams push you forward, but seeing reality clearly is what enables you to turn your dreams into something real.

When you pair bold vision with a grounded understanding of where you are now, you create a path that leads to meaningful success.

The key is not choosing between dreaming and being practical—but learning to balance both. These five questions will help you reflect on your dreams, challenge assumptions, and take confident steps toward your goals.

1. **Am I allowing myself to dream big, or am I limiting my vision based on my current circumstances?**

What would I pursue if I truly believed anything was possible?

2. **Do I have a clear, realistic picture of where I am today?**
   Am I seeing my current situation as it truly is, or am I avoiding difficult truths or making assumptions?

3. **How well do I balance optimism with practical action?**
   Am I taking concrete steps toward my dreams, or am I relying on hope without a strategy?

4. **What's one challenge I've been avoiding because it feels overwhelming?**
   How can I break it down into smaller, manageable steps to keep moving forward?

5. **What's one action I can take today that will bring me closer to my boldest vision?**
   No matter how small, what's a step I can take right now to turn my dream into reality?

THE BOTTOM LINE

Thriving comes from embracing both your dreams and reality.

When you balance optimism with a clear view of the world as it is, you gain the power to make thoughtful, meaningful decisions that move you forward. Facing the facts isn't about giving up on what you hope for—it's about using what's real to build a strong foundation for achieving your goals.

Life rewards those who combine vision with action, hope with practicality.

By seeing things as they truly are, you can make smart choices, overcome challenges, and create the life you've imagined.

It's not about abandoning your dreams; it's about partnering with reality to turn those dreams into something extraordinary. Embrace the journey, trust yourself, and know that you're shaping a future that's as grounded as it is inspiring!

See Clearly And Dream Boldly

Thrive Now!

KEY #6

USE IDENTITY INSTEAD OF WILLPOWER

The fastest way to lasting change is shifting how you see yourself—because when your actions align with your identity, success becomes second nature.

What if creating lasting change didn't have to feel like a constant battle of willpower?

Good news—it doesn't!

There's a better, easier, and more reliable way to make progress: **change who you are and what you focus on rather than just what you** *do*.

In this key I'll show you exactly how to do that.

When you see yourself as the kind of person who naturally makes healthy choices, manages money wisely, or embraces personal growth, the right actions fall into place effortlessly.

Change becomes easier because it's no longer something you have to push yourself to do—it's just part of who you are.

And the best part?

You're not forcing yourself into a version of success that feels unnatural. You're stepping into a more confident, capable, and empowered version of yourself—one that makes progress feel automatic.

Let's find out how to use this key to make change reliable and permanent!

THE WILLPOWER WALL

The Common Grounds Café was bustling with the usual evening crowd, and the four friends had gathered in their familiar corner, cups of coffee steaming in front of them.

The soft hum of conversation and clinking dishes created a warm, comforting atmosphere, but today the energy at the table was tense.

Michael, who normally exuded a calm, steady presence, was visibly frustrated. He stared down at his cup, stirring the coffee absentmindedly.

Emma, always the first to notice when something was off, leaned in. "Alright, Michael. Spill. What's on your mind? You've been stirring that coffee for five minutes."

Michael sighed, setting the spoon down and running a hand through his hair. "I'm just… frustrated. I've been trying so hard to stick to this new routine, but I feel like I'm losing it. I started off strong, but now it's like all my willpower is gone."

Sarah raised an eyebrow. "What are you trying to change?"

"I've been trying to wake up early and hit the gym before work," Michael explained. "The first couple of weeks, I was doing great. I'd force myself out of bed, power through the workout, and I felt good about it. But now… every morning, it's harder to get up. I keep hitting snooze, telling myself 'just five more minutes.' And I've already skipped the gym three times this week."

Jack, sitting across from him, nodded knowingly. "That sounds familiar. I went through the exact same thing when

Use Identity Instead of Willpower

I tried to change my diet. I started strong with willpower, but eventually, it wasn't enough."

Michael's frustration was palpable. "I don't get it. It's like I've run out of fuel. I thought if I just kept pushing through, I'd build the habit, but now I feel like I'm slipping back into my old ways. It's exhausting."

Emma tilted her head. "I think you're hitting the classic willpower wall. It works for a while, but it's not something you can rely on forever. You're running on empty because you're fighting against yourself."

Michael looked up, confused. "What do you mean?"

"It's like this," Sarah chimed in. "I used to rely on willpower all the time when I wanted to change something. But the problem is, willpower is finite. You're expending all this energy trying to force yourself to be someone you're not used to being. At some point, you burn out. The real change happens when you shift how you see yourself—then you've changed your identity, not just your behavior."

Jack nodded. "That's exactly it. When I was struggling with my diet, I was trying to use willpower to resist junk food. And for a while, I was doing okay. But eventually, I'd have a bad day or get stressed, and my willpower would just collapse. What changed for me was when I stopped seeing myself as someone who was *trying* to eat healthy and started seeing myself as someone who *is* healthy."

Michael frowned. "How's that different?"

"It's a big difference," Jack said. "When you're relying on willpower, you're forcing yourself to act against your current identity. You're basically telling yourself, 'I'm not really this person, but I'm going to try to be.' But when you shift your identity—when you start thinking of yourself as someone who is healthy, or in your case, fit—the actions start to flow naturally. It's not a battle every morning. It becomes part of who you are."

Michael sat back, processing Jack's words. "So, you're saying I need to stop seeing myself as someone who's *trying* to work out and start seeing myself as someone who just does it, no question?"

"Exactly," Sarah said. "It's not about waking up and thinking, 'Can I make myself do this today?' It's about waking up and knowing that's just who you are now. You're someone who exercises every day, and that's why you do it—because it's aligned with who you are, not because you're forcing it."

Emma leaned in. "It's all about changing the narrative in your head. Right now, your identity is still wrapped up in your old habits. You're thinking of yourself as someone who has to fight to work out. But if you start seeing yourself as someone who is fit it's natural to work out because that's who you are, you won't have to rely on willpower anymore."

Michael looked thoughtful, the frustration easing from his face a little. "I've never really thought about it like that. I've just been focusing on the action—on dragging myself to the gym every day. But I guess I never tried to change how I see myself in the process."

Use Identity Instead of Willpower

"It's a game changer," Jack said. "Once I started identifying as someone who was healthy, I didn't have to battle with myself every time I walked past a donut. I just didn't want it anymore because it didn't fit with who I was."

Michael nodded slowly. "So, how do I actually change my identity? How do I go from being someone who struggles with this to someone who just *does* it?"

"Make a decision and then use small, consistent actions," Sarah replied. "Start by reinforcing that identity with little wins. Even on days when you don't feel like going to the gym, remind yourself that this is who you are. It's not about perfect execution every time. It's about showing up for yourself, building evidence that you're the kind of person who values fitness. Pretty quickly, it won't feel like a battle anymore."

Michael smiled slightly, a sense of relief washing over him. "I like that. I'm tired of fighting myself every morning. Maybe it's time to change the story I'm telling myself."

Emma raised her cup in a toast. "Here's to dropping the willpower struggle and becoming the person you want to be."

The others lifted your cups in agreement. As they clinked your mugs together, Michael felt a new determination settle in—not the exhausting, push-through-at-all-costs kind of determination, but a deeper, more sustainable belief that he was the person he truly wanted to be.

And this time, he wouldn't rely on willpower to get there.

The café continued to hum with life around them, but at their table, the tension had lifted. Michael knew that his approach had to change.

It wasn't about fighting his way through; it was about becoming someone new—someone who didn't need to rely on willpower to make lasting changes.

WILLPOWER IS A GREAT START

Willpower is a bit like a battery—it starts fully charged, ready to power you through decisions and challenges.

At first, it feels great!

You resist that extra dessert, stick to your workout, or tackle that big project.

But, as you keep relying on it, the battery drains little by little. Suddenly, skipping the workout seems tempting, the project gets postponed, and old habits start creeping back in.

Sound familiar?

Here's the thing: **willpower is an incredible starting tool, but it's not designed to carry you all the way.**

It takes a lot of mental and emotional energy to push against habits, desires, and impulses that have been in place for a long time. And when life gets busy, stressful, or tiring, your willpower naturally fades.

That's why so many people struggle to stick with diets, exercise routines, or new habits—they're relying solely on a resource that wasn't built to last.

Use Identity Instead of Willpower

But why doesn't willpower last?

And more importantly, **what works better?**

Let's take a closer look at how willpower actually works—and how shifting your identity can help you create lasting change without the constant struggle.

WHY WILLPOWER BASED CHANGE IS UNRELIABLE

Ever wonder why so many people struggle to keep their New Year's resolutions?

It's not because they don't want to change—it's because they're relying on willpower alone.

At first, motivation is high. People commit to losing weight, quitting smoking, or getting more organized, and for a little while, they stick with it.

But then, life happens. The motivation fades, willpower runs low, and before they know it, they're slipping back into old habits.

Sound familiar?

That's because **willpower-based change doesn't fix the root of the problem.** It's like trying to drive with the parking brake on—you're using a ton of effort, but something deeper is holding you back.

Willpower is great for short bursts, but it can't rewire deeply ingrained habits—because it doesn't change who you *are*.

And that's where real, lasting change happens.

So instead of forcing yourself to change through sheer effort, **what if you could shift your identity and make the right choices feel natural?**

Let's explore how to do exactly that.

THE POWER OF IDENTITY: THE SECRET TO LASTING CHANGE

If you want to create real, lasting change, **focus on changing your identity—not just your actions.** Your identity shapes your habits, decisions, and behaviors far more than willpower ever could.

> *Your identity is the way you see yourself – how you define who you are at your core.*

At first, the idea of changing your identity might sound overwhelming—but here's the good news: **it's actually easier and more sustainable than constantly forcing yourself to change.**

When you truly see yourself in a certain way, the right actions happen naturally—without needing to rely on motivation or willpower.

Think about it this way: If you see yourself as a healthy person, making healthy choices—like eating nutritious foods or exercising—feels automatic.

You don't have to talk yourself into going to the gym or struggle to resist junk food—**it's just what you do because it's part of who you are.**

Use Identity Instead of Willpower

But if you only see yourself as *someone trying to get healthy,* then every choice becomes a battle. You're constantly fighting against old habits, using willpower to push through, and feeling like change is an uphill struggle.

The key is shifting your identity so that your habits work with you, not against you.

When your identity supports your goals, the process feels natural—because you're not just changing what you do, you're the kind of person who does it effortlessly.

WHY IDENTITY IS SO POWERFUL

Your identity shapes your behavior in ways you might not even realize. **The way you see yourself is an unconscious filter for every decision you make.**

Think about it: if you identify as someone who *"always runs late,"* you'll probably continue to make excuses and rationalize why you can't get places on time.

But when you shift your identity to someone who *"is always on time,"* you'll start planning ahead and prioritizing being on tie without needing to force yourself—it's just what you do.

You naturally start planning ahead, managing your time better, and prioritizing punctuality because that's who you are.

There's no battle, no struggle—just alignment between who you are and how you act.

HOW TO CREATE AND STEP INTO A NEW IDENTITY

Have you ever met someone who just *seems* to have it all together?

The friend who always eats healthy without struggling, the coworker who's effortlessly confident, or the person who manages their money wisely without stressing over every dollar?

The secret isn't willpower—it's **identity.** They don't *try* to be that way. They simply **are** that way. And the good news? **You can do the same.**

Instead of relying on motivation or struggling through habits that don't stick, you can **become** the person who naturally does the things you want to do.

Here's how:

Step 1: Decide What You Want

Before you can become someone new, you have to **decide what you actually want.** Do you want to…

- ☑ Lose weight?
- ☑ Find a life partner?
- ☑ Deepen your friendships?
- ☑ Gain financial independence?

Clarity is key.

The more specific you are about your objective, the easier it is to align your identity with it.

Example: Sarah had struggled with money for years. She wanted to stop feeling stressed about finances and finally start building wealth. Instead of just saying, *"I want to save more money,"* she got clear on what she really wanted: financial independence.

What do <u>you</u> really want?

Step 2: Identify the Key Behavior

Once you know specifically what you want, ask yourself: *What's one key behavior that would naturally lead to this outcome?*

Example: If you want to lose weight, a key behavior could be making mindful food choices.

If you want stronger friendships, it might be reaching out to people regularly. If financial independence is your goal, it could be saving and investing consistently.

This step is about **focusing on the action that truly matters**—the one that, if repeated, would make success inevitable.

For Sarah, the key behavior was simple: spending less than she earned and investing the difference.

Step 3: Turn That Behavior Into an Identity

Now, take that key behavior and turn it into **an identity statement**—a way of describing yourself as if you already *are* the person who achieves that goal.

- **Instead of:** *"I want to lose weight."*
  Say: *"I am someone who weighs 150 pounds."*

- **Instead of:** *"I need to save more money."*
  Say: *"I am someone who has $1,000,000 in their brokerage account."*

- **Instead of:** *"I should work on my friendships."*
  Say: *"I am someone who has deep and meaningful friendships."*

This shift is powerful because **your brain naturally works to stay consistent with your identity.**

When you see yourself as someone who already lives this way, the right behaviors happen naturally.

For Sarah, her new identity was: "I am someone who builds wealth and makes smart financial choices."

Step 4:
Filter Every Decision Through Your New Identity

Now comes the part that makes the real difference: **using your new identity to guide your decisions—both big and small.**

Every time you face a choice, ask yourself:

> *What would someone with this identity do?*

A few examples:

- Would someone who weighs 150 pounds eat this meal?

- Would someone with strong friendships check in on a friend today?

- Would someone who builds wealth buy this expensive gadget on impulse?

Use Identity Instead of Willpower

For Sarah, the next time she was tempted to make an unnecessary purchase, she paused and asked herself:

"Would someone who is becoming financially independent buy this right now?"

That simple question gave her a moment to reflect, helping her make a smarter choice—without feeling like she was depriving herself.

Instead of trying to resist temptation, she was simply acting in alignment with who she was becoming.

Now That's Who You Are!

As you can see, **the key to lasting change isn't forcing yourself into new habits.**

It's stepping into a new version of yourself—one who naturally makes the choices that lead to success. As you make decisions that align with your identity, it becomes automatic!

So, what identity do *you* want to step into?

Start today by deciding what you want, identifying the key behavior, turning it into an identity statement, and filtering your choices through it.

Because when you do this, you *are* the kind of person who does the right things, and success stops being something you chase—it becomes something you *are*.

ARE YOU STUCK TRYING TO USE WILLPOWER?

If you are wondering whether you are relying too much on willpower instead of adopting a more effective identity-based approach to change, here are some questions you can use:

1. **Do I feel like I'm constantly struggling to stick with new habits, only to end up exhausted and frustrated?**
   If the answer is yes, this might indicate a reliance on willpower alone, without shifting underlying beliefs about who you are.

2. **Do I find myself making the same resolutions or goals repeatedly without seeing lasting change?**
   Repeatedly setting the same goals may mean you're focused on temporary efforts rather than an identity shift that would support sustainable change.

3. **When I think about what I want, do I feel like I'm forcing myself to be someone I'm not?**
   If pursuing the change feels unnatural, you may be using willpower rather than aligning your actions with a new identity that naturally supports the goal.

4. **Am I discouraged or overly self-critical if I slip up, rather than seeing it as part of the process?**
   If slipping up makes you feel discouraged or overly self-critical, it may be a sign that you're relying on willpower and perfectionism rather than building an identity that supports lasting change.

When you shift your focus to *being* the kind of person who naturally makes the right choices, setbacks

Use Identity Instead of Willpower

5. **Do I rely on rewards or punishments to stay motivated, rather than feeling genuinely connected to the outcome I am seeking?**
   Relying on external motivators is often a sign that you're not making an internal identity shift, which makes the behavior meaningful and natural instead of forced using motivators.

   The carrot-and-stick approach—rewarding yourself for good behavior and punishing yourself for slip-ups—might work in the short term, but it keeps you in a constant cycle of frustration and chasing motivation instead of making lasting change feel effortless and natural. Eventually you will give up.

6. **Am I avoiding creating systems or environments that support my goal, hoping sheer willpower will carry me through?**
   Avoiding support structures can indicate a willpower-based approach, whereas an identity change often involves setting up systems that align with the person you are.

7. **Do I believe I'll go back to my old ways once I reach my objective, rather than knowing I have made lasting change?**
   If the change feels temporary, it's likely driven by willpower alone. An identity shift makes the new behavior who you are, not just something you're doing for now.

If you answer "yes" to some of these questions, it may be a sign that relying on willpower alone is making change harder than it needs to be.

Focusing on creating a new identity aligned with your goals will make lasting change natural and fulfilling.

MOVE FROM WILLPOWER TO IDENTITY NOW

For years, Sarah relied on sheer willpower to save money. She'd set strict budgets, cut out little luxuries, and promise herself she wouldn't spend impulsively.

And for a while, it worked.

But inevitably, something would happen—a stressful day, an unexpected sale, or just exhaustion from always saying "no"—and she'd fall right back into old spending habits.

That all changed when she stopped relying on willpower and shifted her identity.

Instead of telling herself, *"I need to be better with money,"* she started saying, *"I am someone who builds wealth and makes smart financial choices."*

And with that simple shift, everything started to change.

Instead of resisting impulse purchases, she naturally paused and asked, "Would someone who wants to be financially independent buy this right now?"

The answer was always obvious, and instead of forcing herself to save, she saw it as something she *wanted* to do—because it aligned with who she was.

The same is true for you.

Use Identity Instead of Willpower

When you shift from willpower to identity, the struggle fades. You no longer have to force yourself into the right actions—they simply become part of who you are.

So, what should you do now?

Pick one area of your life and start the shift today.

Decide who you want to become, align your choices with that identity, and let the transformation happen naturally.

BEYOND WILLPOWER
5 QUESTIONS TO CREATE LASTING CHANGE

As you know, willpower can help you start, but identity is what keeps you going.

These five reflection questions will help you shift your mindset and set yourself up for lasting success—without the struggle.

1. **Have I been relying on willpower to make changes, or have I shifted my identity to support them?**
   Am I constantly pushing myself to take action, or does my identity naturally reinforce my goals?

2. **What is one habit I struggle to maintain, and what identity shift would make it feel effortless?**
   For example, instead of forcing myself to work out, how can I start seeing myself as someone who prioritizes fitness?

3. **When I face challenges, do I see them as failures or opportunities to strengthen my new identity?**

Do I get discouraged when I slip up, or do I use it as a learning moment to reinforce who I'm becoming?

4. **What's one decision I can start filtering through my new identity today?**
   For example, if I want to be financially independent, how would a financially responsible person handle this purchase?

5. **Am I waiting to "feel ready" before stepping into my new identity, or am I acting as if I already am that person?**
   What decision can I make today to reinforce my identity and build momentum?

THE BOTTOM LINE

Struggling against your own habits, constantly battling temptation, and relying on sheer determination won't get you where you want to go.

In fact, it's more likely to lead to burnout and frustration—sending you right back to old patterns.

But **real, lasting change doesn't have to be a fight.**

The key isn't more willpower—it's shifting your identity.

When you change the way you see yourself, the actions that once felt difficult become second nature.

Instead of forcing yourself to make the right choices, you'll naturally take the steps that align with the person you're becoming.

Use Identity Instead of Willpower

No struggle.

No exhaustion.

Just real progress toward the thriving life you truly want!

Thrive Now!

Use Identity Instead of Willpower

Thrive Now!

KEY #7

TRANSFORM PAIN INTO POWER

Pain isn't something to avoid—it's a signal guiding you toward growth, strength, and resilience when you learn to listen and transform it into progress.

No one likes pain—it's uncomfortable, and our instinct is to avoid it.

But what if, instead of seeing pain as something to escape, you saw it as a guide?

Pain isn't just there to make you suffer—it's your body and mind's way of saying, **"Pay attention—something needs your focus."**

Whether it's physical discomfort or emotional struggle, paying attention to its message enables you uncover the root cause and take meaningful steps toward healing and growth.

Once you realize this, pain becomes an opportunity—one that leads to greater understanding, resilience, and strength.

By embracing what pain has to offer, you stop feeling powerless and start using it as a tool to create positive change.

Your greatest challenges can become your greatest sources of power—if you're willing to listen and learn.

FACING THE TRUTH

The Common Grounds Café was quieter than usual as the four friends gathered at their favorite corner table.

The early spring sunshine created a soft backdrop to the tension that hung in the air. Sarah sat with her hands wrapped around her coffee cup, staring down at the disappearing foam. Her usual bright energy was noticeably absent, and the others could sense something was off.

Michael glanced at Emma, who gave him a slight nod, as if to encourage him to ask what was wrong. He cleared his throat and leaned forward. "Sarah, you've been pretty quiet today. What's going on? Something's on your mind, isn't it?"

Sarah let out a long sigh, finally looking up at her friends. "Yeah... there's a lot on my mind, actually. I've been feeling so stressed and overwhelmed, and I think I've been avoiding it instead of dealing with the real issue."

Jack, always the first to jump in with support, raised an eyebrow. "What do you mean? What's going on?"

Sarah hesitated, shifting in her seat. "It's my job. I've been unhappy for a while now. It's draining me, and I feel stuck. But instead of dealing with it, I've been distracting myself—binge-watching TV every night, going out just to avoid thinking about it. It's like I'm trying to numb the stress, but it's not working. Every time I come back to reality, the problem's still there."

Emma nodded knowingly. "I get that. It's easy to make that mistake—using distractions to avoid the pain. But the thing is, the pain doesn't go away, right? It just gets louder the longer you ignore it."

Sarah leaned back in her chair, rubbing her temples. "Exactly. I think I've known for a while that this job isn't right for me anymore, but I keep telling myself that maybe things will get better, that I just need to push through. But deep down, I know I'm just avoiding the truth. I'm miserable, and I don't know what to do about it."

Jack leaned in, his voice steady and encouraging. "You know, Sarah, pain is there for a reason. It's like a warning light on your dashboard, telling you something's wrong. Ignoring it doesn't make it go away—it just makes the problem worse. Have you thought about what's really causing the stress? What's the root of it?"

Sarah frowned. "I guess I haven't really faced it head-on. I keep thinking that maybe I'm just burned out, or that everyone feels this way at some point. But if I'm honest with myself... I don't feel fulfilled anymore. I feel like I'm stuck in this job because it's safe, but it's not what I want to do with my life."

Michael nodded thoughtfully. "It sounds like you're at a crossroads, and that's not easy. But avoiding it isn't going to help you move forward. You've been numbing the pain, but maybe it's time to listen to what it's telling you."

Sarah bit her lip, her eyes downcast. "I guess I've been afraid of what it means if I admit I'm unhappy. It feels so overwhelming to think about making a change."

Emma reached across the table, resting her hand on Sarah's. "I know it's scary. But avoiding the pain is only going to keep you stuck. What if you started by just acknowledging the problem, facing it without trying to push it away? What's the worst that could happen if you took a closer look?"

Sarah let out a shaky breath. "I guess... I'd have to admit that I need to make a change. And that terrifies me because I don't know what comes next."

"That's okay," Jack said softly. "You don't have to have it all figured out right away. The first step is just admitting the pain is there for a reason. It's trying to guide you, not punish you. Once you accept that, you can start making decisions that lead you toward something better."

Michael added, "It's like this: you can keep distracting yourself, but the pain will always be waiting for you when you stop. Or you can use it as motivation to finally make the changes you need. Trust me, you'll feel so much better when you're actually addressing the problem, not running from it."

Sarah looked up at her friends, their encouragement starting to seep in. "You're right. I've been avoiding it because I don't want to deal with the uncertainty. But I can't keep numbing myself forever. I have to face this, even if it's scary."

Emma smiled. "Exactly. You've already taken the hardest step by recognizing that you've been avoiding the pain. Now, it's about finding a way forward. We've got your back."

Jack lifted his cup. "To facing the pain and using it to make life better."

The others raised their cups, clinking them together in solidarity. Sarah smiled, feeling a small sense of relief wash over her.

She knew the journey ahead might be challenging, but with her friends' support—and a new perspective on pain—she was ready to stop running and start facing her problems head-on.

As The sunshine warmed the room, the tension begun to lift.

Sarah realized that the pain she had been avoiding wasn't something to fear—it was something to listen to, something that could guide her toward the changes she needed to make.

THE PURPOSE OF PAIN: A CALL TO ACTION

Believe it or not, **pain is here to help you.**

It's like a friendly nudge (or sometimes a blaring alarm) saying, "Hey, something needs your attention!"

Whether it's physical or emotional, **pain is your body and mind's built-in warning system, designed to protect and guide you.**

Physical pain tells you that your body needs care—maybe you've pushed too hard, or there's an injury that needs attention.

Emotional pain works the same way.

It signals that something in your life—a relationship, a job, or a habit—may need to change.

Instead of being something to fear or ignore, pain is a messenger helping you recognize areas that need care, reflection, and action.

Imagine ignoring the pain of a broken ankle and continuing to walk on it. You wouldn't heal—you'd make things worse.

And emotional pain is no different.

Avoiding the discomfort of a toxic relationship, a stressful job, or unresolved emotions doesn't make them disappear—it only compounds the stress and spreads into other areas of your life.

Here's the good news: **When you stop seeing pain as something to escape and start seeing it as a signal, you unlock its purpose.**

Pain isn't here to hold you back—it's here to guide you toward healing, growth, and positive change.

Instead of resisting it, listen.

What is your pain trying to tell you? What action can you take to resolve it?

Pain isn't your enemy—it's your teacher.

And when you embrace its lessons, you gain the insight, strength, and motivation to build a healthier, happier, and more fulfilling life.

Let pain be the spark that leads to transformation!

HOW PEOPLE AVOID PAIN
(AND WHY AVOIDING DOESN'T WORK)

Let's be honest—**no one enjoys pain.**

It's uncomfortable, sometimes overwhelming, and our natural instinct is to escape it. That's why people go to great lengths to numb, distract, or avoid pain rather than facing it head-on.

But here's the truth: **avoiding pain doesn't make it disappear—it just delays the inevitable.** And often, the longer you avoid it, the bigger it grows.

Here are some of the most common ways people try to escape discomfort—and why these coping mechanisms often create even more pain in the long run.

Numbing with Food, Alcohol, or Drugs

When emotions feel too heavy, many people turn to food, alcohol, or substances to take the edge off. That extra slice of cake, the second (or third) glass of wine, or even relying on prescription medication can provide temporary relief.

But the pain doesn't go away—it just gets buried temporarily. And it will probably come back stronger once the numbing wears off.

Over time, emotional eating, excessive drinking, or substance use can lead to health problems, regret, and a deeper sense of disconnection from what's really causing the pain.

Procrastination and Avoidance

Dreading a tough conversation? Facing a financial mess? Struggling in a relationship? Procrastination makes it easy to pretend the problem isn't there—for a while.

The problem?

Pain doesn't magically disappear when you ignore it.

Bills pile up, relationships deteriorate, and the stress of avoiding the problem often becomes worse than facing it.

Constant Distractions (Social Media, TV, etc.)

Scrolling through social media, binge-watching TV shows, or diving into video games feels like an escape, but it's really just a delay.

Distractions might help in the moment, but once the screen turns off, the pain is still there—unresolved, waiting for you.

Instead of truly relaxing, these avoidance tactics often leave people feeling drained and unfulfilled.

Overworking

Some people avoid pain by throwing themselves into work. Staying busy, chasing deadlines, and focusing on career achievements can feel productive—but when it's used as an escape, burnout is inevitable.

No amount of success at work can make up for unresolved personal struggles. Eventually, the exhaustion catches up, and the pain you've been avoiding demands your attention.

People-Pleasing

Saying "yes" when you really want to say "no." Avoiding conflict to keep the peace. Putting everyone else's needs ahead of your own.

People-pleasing often comes from a fear of rejection or conflict, but it creates internal pain in the form of resentment, exhaustion, and frustration.

At first, it might seem easier to keep everyone happy—but over time, neglecting your own needs leads to even deeper struggles.

FACE PAIN AND TAKE BACK YOUR POWER

Avoiding pain keeps you stuck.

But when you learn to face it, listen to what it's telling you, and take action, you **turn pain into a powerful tool for growth.**

Instead of asking, *"How can I escape this?"* start asking, *"What is this trying to teach me?"*

The sooner you stop running from pain, the sooner you can move forward—stronger, wiser, and more in control of your life.

ARE YOU AVOIDING PAIN?

If you want to truly thrive, it's time to stop seeing pain as something to escape and start seeing it as a valuable teacher.

Pain isn't just discomfort—it's information.

It's trying to tell you something.

When you acknowledge it, identify the root cause, and take responsibility for making changes, you turn pain into a powerful force for growth and transformation.

Instead of avoiding the discomfort, let it guide you. The very thing you're avoiding might be the key to healing, strength, and success.

7 Questions to Help You Find Out

These seven questions will help you recognize whether you're unintentionally avoiding pain and, more importantly, how you can start turning it into a source of strength, clarity, and progress.

1. **Do I distract myself with food, entertainment, work, or other habits instead of addressing difficult emotions or challenges?**
   When something feels uncomfortable, do I immediately reach for my phone, grab a snack, or bury myself in work rather than dealing with the real issue?

2. **Is there an uncomfortable truth I've been avoiding because facing it feels too difficult?**
   Maybe it's a relationship that isn't working, a job that's draining you, or a personal habit that's holding you back.

3. **Do I put off difficult decisions, hoping the situation will resolve itself?**
   Am I delaying action because it feels overwhelming, even though deep down I know avoiding it only makes things worse?

4. **Do I ignore or downplay feelings of stress, frustration, or unhappiness instead of exploring where they're coming from?**
   Am I convincing myself "it's not that bad" when, in reality, something clearly needs to change?

5. **Have I been making excuses for staying in a situation that no longer serves me?**
   Am I justifying staying stuck—telling myself it's "too late" to change, or that things will "magically" get better?

6. **Do I struggle to have honest conversations about my needs, boundaries, or concerns?**
   Am I avoiding difficult conversations because I fear conflict or discomfort, even when speaking up could ultimately improve the situation?

7. **What's one thing I've been avoiding because it feels uncomfortable—but deep down, I know addressing it would help me grow?**
   What step can I take today to start facing it?

Your Next Step:
Face It, Learn from It, and Move Forward

If you recognize yourself in any of these questions, you're not alone.

Everybody avoids pain in different ways—but the good news is, you have the power to shift.

Instead of running from discomfort, pause and listen to what it's telling you. What is your pain trying to teach you? What would happen if you faced it head-on?

The moment you stop avoiding pain is the moment you take back control of your growth, your life, and your future.

HOW TO USE PAIN AS A MOTIVATOR FOR CHANGE

Pain is often seen as something to escape—but **what if you could use it to your advantage?**

Take Amelia, for example. She had been unhappy in her job for years, feeling undervalued and stuck, but she kept pushing those feelings aside.

She told herself she should be grateful for a stable paycheck, even though every Sunday night filled her with dread.

Instead of listening to what her discomfort was telling her, she numbed it—staying busy, distracting herself with social media, Netflix, a few glasses of wine, and telling herself *"it's just work, everyone feels this way."*

But deep down, she knew the truth: **her pain was trying to tell her something.**

One day, after yet another exhausting week, she decided to stop ignoring it. She asked herself: What is this discomfort trying to teach me?

That's when everything changed.

Transform Pain into Power

Sarah's story is a perfect example of how pain can be used not as a roadblock, but as a catalyst for action. Here's how you can do the same:

Acknowledge the Pain

The first step is to **stop running from it.** Avoiding or suppressing pain only delays healing. Recognize that pain isn't your enemy—it's a message.

Do this: Take a deep breath and say to yourself, "I am feeling pain, and that's okay." The moment you acknowledge it, you begin to take back control.

Example: Amelia admitted to herself that her job was draining her, instead of pretending everything was fine.

Identify the Source of the Pain

Pain doesn't appear out of nowhere.

What's causing it?

Is it a specific situation, relationship, or habit? Once you pinpoint the source, you can start working toward change.

Do this: Ask yourself, "What is causing this pain?" Write down the situations that trigger discomfort and look for patterns.

If you need help identifying the cause of the pain, ash yourself "What happens right before I feel this way?"

Example: Amelia realized it wasn't just her job itself—it was the lack of growth, lack of appreciation, and the feeling that she was settling for less than she deserved.

Face the Pain Head-On (Even When It Feels Scary)

Let's be honest—facing pain isn't easy.

It can feel overwhelming, uncomfortable, and even scary to acknowledge what's really going on. That's why so many people push it aside, hoping it will fade on its own. But, as you know, avoiding pain doesn't make it disappear—it only allows it to grow.

The truth is, **the fear of facing pain is often worse than the pain itself.** Once you acknowledge it, you regain control, and the path forward becomes clearer.

Do this: When you feel the urge to distract yourself, pause and ask, "If I don't address this, where will I be in a year? In five years?"

Example: Amelia had been unhappy in her job for years, but the idea of change felt daunting. Then she imagined staying in the same role for five more years—waking up every day dreading work, feeling undervalued, and watching opportunities pass her by. **That realization was more painful than facing the discomfort of making a change.**

Yes, facing pain is hard—but staying stuck is even harder. When you acknowledge what's holding you back, you take the first step toward freedom, growth, and a better future.

See Pain as an Opportunity for Growth

Pain isn't here to punish you—it's pointing you toward something better. Instead of seeing it as an obstacle, ask what lesson it's teaching you.

Transform Pain into Power

Do this: Ask yourself, "How can this pain help me grow? What changes is it pushing me to make?"

Example: Amelia realized that her frustration was actually a sign that she was ready for something bigger. Instead of seeing it as suffering that had to be endured, she saw it as motivation to take action.

Accept That Pain is Part of Life

It's not something we enjoy, but it's part of being human. The sooner you accept that pain will come and go, the less power it has over you.

Do this: When pain arises, instead of resisting it, sit with it. Let yourself feel it without judgment, and remind yourself that it's temporary.

Example: Amelia stopped feeling guilty about her dissatisfaction and started seeing it as a natural signal for growth.

Take Responsibility for Change

You may not control everything that happens to you, but **you always control your response.** Once you acknowledge what needs to change, commit to taking action.

Do this: Identify one step you can take to address the root cause of your pain. For more about this see *Turn Challenge Into Choice* on page 193.

Example: Amelia didn't quit her job immediately, but she started updating her resume, networking, and researching new opportunities. She took ownership of her future instead of waiting for things to change on their own.

Create and Execute a Plan for Change

Once you've faced your pain, **turn it into action.**

What steps can you take to address the root cause?

Whether it's a relationship, career, or personal struggle, having a clear plan makes change feel achievable.

Do this: Write down three concrete steps you can take to move forward.

Example: Amelia's plan was simple:

1. Update her resume and LinkedIn profile.
2. Apply for at least three jobs per week.
3. Practice interview skills with a friend.

Celebrate Progress—No Matter How Small

Change doesn't always happen overnight, but **every action you take matters.** Recognizing your progress keeps you motivated and reinforces your new mindset.

Do this: Keep a journal of small wins. Each time you make progress—no matter how minor—celebrate it.

Example: Amelia didn't wait until she got a new job to celebrate. She wrote down her progress every time she sent out a resume, made a new connection, or improved her skills.

THE BOTTOM LINE: USE PAIN AS YOUR FUEL

Pain isn't here to hold you back—it's here to push you forward. Instead of avoiding it, listen to it, learn from it, and let it motivate you.

Transform Pain into Power

Just like Amelia, you can take control of your life by acknowledging your pain, facing it head-on, and using it as a tool for transformation.

The moment you stop running from discomfort is the moment you take back your power.

KEY #8

TURN CHALLENGE INTO CHOICE

You can't control everything that happens, but you can control how you respond—this key shows you how to turn obstacles into opportunities by owning your reactions.

Life will always throw challenges your way—some small, some life-altering. But your greatest strength isn't in avoiding difficulties—it's in choosing on purpose how you respond to them.

While you can't control everything that happens, you always have control over your response. And that's where your real power lies.

When faced with a tough conversation, a stressful situation at work, or an unexpected financial setback, it's easy to feel stuck or overwhelmed.

But shifting your focus to what _you_ can do puts in control and sets you up for getting what you want in life.

Turn Challenge Into Choice

Instead of feeling trapped by external circumstances, you step into a position of strength, where you can create solutions, grow, and move forward.

Owning your emotions and actions means you no longer let life—or other people—decide your happiness for you. You reclaim your power by saying, "This is my life, and I choose how I respond."

Every response you make is an opportunity—to shape your path, build resilience, and take control of your future.

It's not just about reacting—it's about making intentional choices that align with the life you want to create.

When you take ownership of your responses, you unlock the ability to thrive, no matter what life throws your way.

TAKING BACK CONTROL

The late afternoon sun streamed through the windows of The Common Grounds Café, casting long shadows on the wooden floor as the familiar group of four sat around their usual table.

The atmosphere was cozy, as always, but today there was an undeniable tension. Sarah slumped in her chair, her arms crossed tightly across her chest, staring down at her untouched coffee.

Jack leaned forward, concern etched across his face. "Sarah, you're pretty quiet today. What's going on?"

Sarah let out a deep sigh. "It's just been…one of those weeks." She shook her head, clearly frustrated. "I can't catch a break. My boss completely undermined me in front of the whole team—took credit for a project I spent months working on. It was humiliating."

Emma frowned sympathetically. "That's awful. I can't believe your boss did that."

"I know, right?" Sarah's voice rose, her frustration bubbling over. "And it's not the first time. It's like no matter how hard I work, someone else just swoops in and takes the credit. It's unfair, and I'm just…done with it. What's the point of even trying when someone else is always going to steal your thunder?"

Michael, who had been listening quietly, spoke up. "It sucks when things like that happen. But what are you going to do about it?"

Turn Challenge Into Choice

Sarah blinked, clearly taken aback. "What do you mean, 'What am I going to do about it?' There's *nothing* I *can* do. It's out of my hands. My boss is in charge and he can do whatever he wants. I'm just stuck dealing with it."

Jack leaned back in his chair, shaking his head. "I get where you're coming from, but it sounds like you're giving up all your power here. I mean, sure, you can't control what your boss did, but you can control how you respond to it."

Sarah frowned. "How am I supposed to respond to being treated like garbage? It's not like I can just make it go away."

"Maybe not," Emma said gently. "But the way you're talking about it—like you're powerless—that's only going to keep you feeling frustrated and angry. I'm not saying it wasn't unfair, but right now, you're letting this situation control you. You have more options than you think."

Sarah huffed. "Like what? Quit my job? That's not exactly realistic."

Michael smiled slightly. "Maybe not quit right now, but you can stand up for yourself. You can talk to your boss, set boundaries, or even start exploring other job opportunities if this isn't the right place for you. What you *can't* do is keep giving your power away by saying there's nothing you can do."

Jack nodded. "Exactly. You're focusing so much on what your boss did, but what about how you're handling it? Right now, you're stuck in this victim mindset, and trust me, I've been there. It feels like the world's just happening to you, and you've got no control. But that's not true. You always have control over how you respond."

Sarah sighed again, this time softer. "So, what? I'm supposed to just pretend it didn't bother me?"

"No," Emma said firmly. "It's okay to be upset. What happened wasn't fair, and you have every right to feel how you feel. But once you've felt it, you've got to ask yourself what comes next. How are you going to handle this situation in a way that empowers you, not keeps you stuck?"

Michael leaned in. "Look, Sarah. I know it's easier to just stay mad and complain. We've all been there. But that won't help you. You need to focus on what's within your control. Maybe it's having a conversation with your boss about how you feel. Maybe it's deciding to let this slide but learning how to protect your work better next time. Either way, you get to choose how you respond."

Sarah stared down at her coffee, her shoulders slumped. "I guess I just feel so tired of fighting. It's like no matter what I do, I can't win."

"That's the thing," Jack said softly. "Winning doesn't always mean changing what happens to you. Sometimes, winning is just about how you handle it. You can't control your boss, but you *can* control whether you let them get to you. You choose to take your power back by focusing on what's next instead of what happened."

Sarah was quiet for a long moment, her friends' words sinking in. "I've been stuck in this headspace, thinking I'm powerless," she admitted, her voice softer now. "But maybe... maybe I'm giving up too easily. Maybe I need to stop focusing on what I can't change and start focusing on what I can."

Emma smiled, reaching out to give her hand a supportive squeeze. "Exactly. You've got more control than you think. You just have to take it."

Sarah smiled faintly, feeling a shift in perspective beginning to take hold. "I guess I've been so focused on what went wrong that I didn't even think about how I could make it right. Maybe I should talk to my boss or, at the very least, figure out how to protect my work better."

Michael raised his cup in a toast. "That's the spirit. Here's to taking back control—no more victim mindset."

The others clinked your cups together, the atmosphere around the table lightening.

Sarah still felt the sting of what had happened, but, for the first time in a while, she also felt empowered. She knew now that while she couldn't always control what life threw her way, she had full control over how she responded to it. And that, in itself, was a victory.

As they continued to chat, the sense of frustration began to melt away.

Sarah left the café that day with a renewed sense of purpose, ready to reclaim her power and tackle the situation on her own terms.

It wasn't about changing what had happened—it was about changing her response, and in doing so, changing her outlook on everything that came next.

TAKING BACK YOUR POWER: OWNING YOUR RESPONSE FEELS WONDERFUL

Let's be honest—blaming someone or something else can feel like a relief in the moment.

"This isn't my fault!" is an easy way to let yourself off the hook.

And sometimes, it really *isn't* your fault.

But here's the exciting truth: **even when something isn't your fault, your power lies in how you respond.**

When you take ownership of your reactions, you reclaim control over your life.

Instead of waiting for other people to change or hoping circumstances magically improve (which they probably won't), you put yourself in a position of strength. You stop feeling stuck, frustrated, or powerless because you're the one creating solutions and moving forward.

Sure, blaming external factors might feel good temporarily—but it also keeps you trapped.

It ties you to things you can't control, and that feels terrible. Shifting your focus inward—on what *you* can do—opens the door to clarity, action, and real change.

This isn't about ignoring challenges—it's about stepping into your power.

By choosing how you respond, you align you make progress no matter what life throws your way.

And here's the best part: each time you take ownership of your response, you're not just improving your situation—

you're building resilience, confidence, and a deep sense of control over your happiness and success.

Now *that's* a choice worth celebrating!

FOCUSING ON WHAT YOU CAN CONTROL: A PATH TO THRIVING

One of the most powerful shifts you can make in life is **learning the difference between what you can control and what you can't.**

Once you understand this, you stop wasting energy on things outside your influence and start focusing on actions that actually move you forward.

While you may not always control what happens—whether it's other people's actions, unexpected setbacks, or life's surprises—you <u>always</u> have control over how you interpret and respond to those events.

And that's where your true power lies.

Meet Daniel:
A Lesson in Letting Go of the Uncontrollable

Daniel had spent weeks preparing for a big client presentation for his new agency.

He had rehearsed every word, double-checked the details, and felt confident walking into the meeting. But then—everything fell apart.

The client's priorities had shifted at the last minute. They barely engaged with his proposal, and before he even finished, they shut the whole idea down.

At first, Daniel was furious. How could they dismiss his hard work so easily?

His mind raced with frustration:

- ☑ *If only they had given me more time.*
- ☑ *If only I had known their needs had changed.*
- ☑ *If only I could go back and do it differently.*

But then, he caught himself.

He couldn't change what had happened—but he *could* control what happened next.

Instead of dwelling on what went wrong, he asked himself:

- ☑ *What can I learn from this?*
- ☑ *How can I adjust for the future?*
- ☑ *What's my next best step?*

Instead of leaving defeated, he chose to follow up with the client, ask thoughtful questions about their new priorities, and use that information to refine his next approach.

He walked away stronger, more prepared, and in control of his next move.

Meet Mark:
Letting Go Of A Relationship

Mark had always been the kind of person who liked to fix things.

When his girlfriend, Emily, started pulling away and becoming distant, he did everything he could to bring them back to how they used to be.

He planned thoughtful dates, sent sweet messages, and even tried to have deep conversations about what was wrong. But no matter what he did, Emily seemed emotionally checked out.

At first, Mark felt frustrated and hurt.

What had changed? Wasn't he doing everything right? He found himself overanalyzing their conversations, trying to control the outcome, and hoping that if he just tried harder, things would go back to normal.

Then one evening, after another one-sided conversation, it hit him.

He couldn't control Emily's feelings. He couldn't force her to be engaged in the relationship. The only thing he had control over was himself—his emotions, his actions, and his choices.

Instead of chasing after something that wasn't working, **he chose to shift his focus.** He stopped trying to "fix" things that were beyond his control and instead asked himself:

- ☑ *Am I happy in this relationship as it is right now?*
- ☑ *Am I being treated with the same love and effort I give?*
- ☑ *What do I truly want in a partner?*

For the first time in months, he felt relief.

He realized that **holding onto something that wasn't working wasn't love—it was fear.** Fear of change, fear of letting go, fear of the unknown.

So instead of trying to control the situation, he made a choice—to **let go with grace.** He had an honest conversation with Emily, told her he valued their time together but needed to be in a relationship where both people were fully invested, and then he walked away.

It wasn't easy, but it was empowering.

By focusing on what he *could* control—his own choices—he opened the door to a future where he wasn't waiting for someone else to decide his happiness.

WHY THIS SHIFT MATTERS

Focusing on what you can control:

- Frees you from frustration – No more wasting energy on things beyond your reach.
- Opens the door to action – You stop feeling stuck and start making progress.
- Builds confidence and resilience – You realize that no matter what happens, you have the ability to navigate it.

The truth is life will always bring challenges.

But when you focus on what's within your control, you grow, adapt, and thrive—no matter what comes your way.

And that's where real power begins.

CHANGE INTO CHOICE IN ACTION: A TALE OF TWO CHOICES

Jake and Ryan both worked at the same company and were up for a long-awaited promotion.

Both had put in extra hours, taken on challenging projects, and felt confident that they were the best fit for the role.

Then, the news came: neither of them got the promotion. The position had been given to someone from outside the company.

Both men were frustrated. But what happened next was completely different.

Jake spent the next few weeks feeling bitter. He ranted to his coworkers, replayed the decision in his head, and convinced himself that his efforts had been wasted. "What's the point of working so hard if they're just going to overlook me?" he muttered.

His motivation took a hit.

He did his job but stopped going the extra mile. He checked LinkedIn constantly, looking for jobs but never actually applying—because deep down, he felt stuck.

He was waiting for circumstances to change instead of taking action.

Ryan was just as disappointed, but instead of staying stuck, he asked himself better questions. (To learn how to ask better questions, see page 89.)

Instead of checking out, he checked in with his manager. He asked for feedback on what he could improve. He enrolled in an online leadership course. He even started networking with people in his industry.

And then, six months later—a new opportunity opened up.

Because Ryan had been actively improving himself and making connections, he wasn't just considered—he was offered a leadership role that actually paid more than the one he initially wanted.

The Power of Choice

The difference between Jake and Ryan wasn't in the challenge—it was in how they chose to respond.

Jake focused on what he couldn't change. Ryan focused on what he could.

Your choices matter.

When you shift your energy from frustration to action, from waiting to creating, you take back control of your future.

ARE YOU GIVING AWAY CONTROL OF YOUR LIFE?

Life doesn't always go as planned, and sometimes, challenges arise that you didn't ask for or expect.

But the real question isn't about what happened—it's about what you do next.

Are you taking charge of your responses and shaping your path forward, or are you unknowingly giving away your power?

Here are some questions to help you reflect on where you're standing and how you can step into a more empowered mindset.

1. **Am I focusing more on what happened to me, or on what I can do to address the situation?**
   If you're replaying the event in your mind but not taking

action, you may be stuck in reaction mode instead of taking control of your next steps.

2. **Do I blame other people or circumstances for how I feel or where I am in life?**
   Blaming external factors might feel justified and you might even be right, but it also keeps you stuck. Taking ownership of your emotions and actions puts you back in control.

3. **Am I letting my emotions dictate my actions, or am I pausing to reflect before choosing how to respond?**
   Reacting impulsively will usually make situations worse. Slowing down and choosing your response allows you to act from a place of strength rather than emotion.

4. **When something goes wrong, do I ask myself, 'What can I learn from this?' or 'How can I grow from this experience?'**
   Viewing setbacks as lessons rather than roadblocks is a sign that you're taking responsibility for your personal growth.

5. **Am I regularly addressing problems head-on, even when it's uncomfortable, or do I avoid them and hope they go away?**
   Facing challenges directly means you're owning your role in shaping your future, while avoidance often leads to even bigger problems down the road.

6. **Do I focus on what I can control in difficult situations, or do I spend more time worrying about things beyond my control?**
   Worrying about things you can't change drains your energy. Focusing on what's within your control is a key indicator of an empowered mindset.

7. **Am I actively working to improve or change areas of my life that aren't working, or do I feel stuck and powerless?**
   Feeling stuck can signal a victim mindset, while taking even small steps toward improvement shows that you're reclaiming your power.

Taking Back Control Starts Now

If you found yourself answering "no" or "I'm not sure" to some of these questions, that's okay. The fact that you're reflecting on them is already a step toward change.

Empowerment isn't about controlling everything because that's certainly not possible or even desirable—it's about owning your reactions, making intentional choices, and taking action to create the life you want.

TURNING CHALLENGE INTO CHOICE: HOW TO TAKE BACK YOUR POWER

Life is full of challenges—some small, some life-changing. But here's the key difference between staying stuck and moving forward: It's not what happens to you; it's how you respond.

Here's how to turn any challenge into a choice:

Turn Challenge Into Choice

Describe the Challenge

Before you can solve a problem, **you need to get clear on what it is.** A vague sense of frustration won't help—you need to name the challenge and define exactly what's happening.

What to do: Take a step back and describe the challenge as factually as possible. Avoid exaggerating or adding emotions just yet—stick to the details.

Example: Olivia was excited about a big work project, but at the last minute, her manager gave it to someone else without explanation. Now, she feels overlooked and unappreciated.

Describe How It Makes You Feel

Next, **acknowledge your emotions.** It's normal to feel frustrated, disappointed, or even angry when things don't go your way.

Do this: Take a moment to name your feelings. Are you upset? Hurt? Resentful? Recognizing how you feel helps you process emotions instead of letting them control you.

Example: Olivia realizes she feels frustrated and undervalued. She worked hard on this project, and now she's questioning whether her efforts even matter.

Determine Whether This Emotion Serves You

Now ask yourself: Does this emotion serve me well?

Some emotions—like determination or healthy frustration—can fuel growth. Others—like resentment or blame—can keep you stuck.

What to do: If your emotion motivates you to take action, keep it! But if it's keeping you stuck, it's time to shift gears.

Example: Olivia realizes that staying frustrated won't change the situation. It's only making her feel powerless. She decides to shift her focus.

Focus on What You Can Control

Instead of getting stuck on what's unfair or out of your control, **zero in on what you CAN change.**

What to do: Make two lists—one for what you can control and one for what you can't. Then, put all your energy into the first list.

Example: Olivia can't control her manager's decision, but she *can* control how she responds. She can seek feedback, improve her visibility at work, and position herself for the next big opportunity.

Ask the Right Questions

Instead of asking unhelpful questions like, *"Why does this always happen to me?"* shift to empowering questions that guide you toward solutions.

What to do: Ask empowering questions such as these:

- What is one thing I can do right now to improve this situation?
- How can I turn this setback into an opportunity?
- If I were giving advice to a friend in this situation, what would I tell them?
- What will I think about this situation a year from now?

- What's my next step?

Example: Olivia asks herself, "What can I do to make sure my contributions are recognized next time?" This question leads her to set up a meeting with her manager to discuss future opportunities.

Let Go of Blame

Blaming others—even when they are at fault—keeps you stuck. Shifting your focus from blame to responsibility gives you back your power.

What to do: If you catch yourself blaming someone, stop and ask, *"How can I take responsibility for moving forward?"*

Example: Olivia could spend weeks resenting her manager, but that won't help her career. Instead, she focuses on what she can do to make herself stand out moving forward.

Find the Lesson

Every challenge holds a lesson—if you're willing to look for it. What can this experience teach you that will help you grow?

What to do: Ask yourself:

- ☑ What did this challenge teach me?
- ☑ How can I use this lesson to succeed in the future?

Example: Olivia realized that she needs to be more vocal about her contributions and take initiative in meetings. So, moving forward she makes sure her efforts are seen, which leads to bigger opportunities.

THE BOTTOM LINE

Thriving isn't about having a perfect life—it's about recognizing the **incredible power you already have** to shape your future.

While you can't always control what happens, **you can always control how you respond**—and that's where real transformation begins.

When you take ownership of your emotions, choose empowering responses, and focus on what's within your control, **you stop feeling like life is happening to you and start creating the life you want.**

Instead of waiting for circumstances to change and life to happen to you, **you take action, make choices, and move forward with confidence.**

By embracing responsibility for your reactions, **you unlock your full potential.**

You become the kind of person who faces challenges head-on, learns from setbacks, and takes charge of your own success.

The power to thrive is in your choices—make wise choices.

Turn Challenge Into Choice

BRINGING IT ALL TOGETHER

CONGRATULATIONS!

What an incredible accomplishment—you've finished the book, and that's something to celebrate!

You've taken the time to reflect, learn, and invest in yourself, and that alone sets you apart. It's proof that you're committed to growth, change, and taking charge of your future.

By reaching this point **you've proven to yourself that you have the determination to follow through.** That's the exact quality that fuels meaningful change and success.

Take a moment to appreciate how far you've come.

This isn't just the end of a book; it's the beginning of an exciting new chapter in your life. Everything you've learned here is a powerful toolkit to help you move forward with confidence and purpose.

Now, it's time to take those insights and put them into action. You're ready, you're capable, and you're unstoppable.

Let's make it happen—you've got this!

Congratulations!

A FULL CIRCLE MOMENT AT THE COMMON GROUNDS CAFÉ

The familiar hum of chatter and the comforting aroma of freshly brewed coffee filled the Common Grounds Café.

Once again at their favorite corner table, Emma, Sarah, Michael, and Jack leaned in close, sharing updates on their lives. The table had four half-empty mugs and was scattered with notebooks, but the energy was anything but casual—it was celebratory.

"You know," Emma began, swirling her chai latte, "I can't believe how much has changed since we started having these talks. Remember when I was stuck in that short-term thinking loop, panicking over every little work decision?" She chuckled. "I actually lengthened by time horizon when deciding whether to take on my last new project. Thinking about how I'd feel about it in ten months made me realize it was worth saying yes, even though it's a bit daunting now."

"That's amazing!" Sarah exclaimed. "I was just telling Michael about my own breakthrough. You all remember how I used to mistake being busy for being productive? I've started identifying one big thing each day that really moves the needle. Like yesterday, instead of rearranging my files for the millionth time, I finally sent out the pitch I'd been avoiding. And guess what? They loved it!"

Jack raised his mug in a toast. "Cheers to you both! Honestly, the biggest shift for me was learning to ask better questions. I've stopped beating myself up with, 'Why can't I figure this out?' and instead I ask, 'What's one small step I can take?' It's changed the way I tackle everything—work, relationships, even my health."

Michael nodded. "That's huge, Jack. For me, it was about balancing passion with practicality. You all know how I was trying to make my hobby my whole life, even though it wasn't sustainable. Now I've started carving out dedicated time for it, but I'm also focusing on building a more stable foundation. And guess what? I'm actually enjoying both more than ever."

"That's what it's all about," Emma said, leaning back with a satisfied smile. "Not perfection, but progress. And honestly, I couldn't have done it without this group. You all gave me the clarity and courage to face things I'd been avoiding for years."

Sarah grinned. "Same here. It's like we're each building the life we've wanted all along, one intentional step at a time."

Jack clinked his mug against theirs. "To intentional living—and to this table, where it all started."

Congratulations!

They laughed, the sound filling the cozy café.

It wasn't just the coffee or the camaraderie; it was the realization that their conversations had transformed their lives in ways they couldn't have imagined.

Each of them had faced challenges, learned from mistakes, and taken ownership of their futures—and they had done it together.

As they gathered their things and stepped out into the crisp evening air, the sense of possibility was unmistakable. They weren't just thriving individually—they were thriving together.

HERE'S WHAT WE'VE EXPLORED

Throughout these chapters, we've uncovered eight key areas where small shifts can create big, positive changes in your life—making decisions with a longer time horizon, focusing on meaningful results, asking powerful questions, embracing challenges, balancing passion with practicality, understanding reality, building habits beyond willpower, and taking ownership of your actions.

Each concept has given you tools to move forward with clarity, confidence, and purpose.

The most exciting part?

These ideas are all about thriving, not just surviving.

You've learned that while you can't control everything that happens, you *can* control how you respond, how you think, and how you take action.

This is the foundation for a life of fulfillment, growth, and success.

By applying what you've discovered, you're taking charge of your journey and setting yourself up to thrive in ways that truly matter.

The power is yours—now it's time to make it happen!

THE POWER OF SHIFTING YOUR MINDSET

At the heart of thriving is the realizing that your mindset shapes your reality.

It's the lens through which you navigate life's challenges and opportunities, and it holds the key to whether you feel stuck or empowered.

By choosing to take responsibility for your thoughts, actions, and emotions, you unlock the ability to create a life filled with purpose, progress, and fulfillment.

Let's revisit the key ideas from this book and how they can guide you toward an extraordinary future:

- **Thinking Long-Term:** Making decisions with a long time horizon helps you build a life of intention and avoid impulsive choices. By focusing on the big picture, you create a path toward lasting success.

- **Focusing on What Matters:** Recognizing the difference between activity and results ensures your efforts are directed toward meaningful progress. It's not about doing more—it's about doing what truly matters.

- **Asking Better Questions:** Empowering questions open the door to creative solutions and meaningful action. By

Congratulations!

asking the right questions, you guide your life toward clarity and opportunity.

- **Balancing Passion with Practicality:** Pursuing your passion with purpose and practicality aligns your dreams with real, achievable results. Sometimes, it's the effort behind the scenes that paves the way for your biggest wins.

- **Embracing Reality:** Accepting things as they are gives you the clarity and focus to make smarter decisions. Facing the truth empowers you to take meaningful steps forward.

- **Shaping Your Identity:** When you shift your identity rather than relying on willpower, lasting change becomes effortless. By seeing yourself as the person you want to become, your actions naturally align with your goals.

- **Growing Through Challenges:** Facing pain head-on is a powerful catalyst for growth. Pain is a signal—not something to avoid—that can inspire meaningful change and help you emerge stronger.

- **Owning Your Reactions:** Taking responsibility for how you respond to life's events empowers you to move forward with confidence. You may not control everything that happens, but you always control your response—and that's where your true power lies.

With these insights, you have the tools to shift your mindset, overcome challenges, and create the life you've envisioned.

Each decision, each action, and each moment is an opportunity to step into your power and thrive. You've got this!

THE BENEFITS OF EMBRACING RESPONSIBILITY

When you start applying the ideas from this book to your life, you'll quickly see incredible shifts take place.

One of the most rewarding changes is the clarity and purpose that come from thinking long-term and taking intentional action.

You'll feel energized as you focus on what truly matters, leaving distractions behind and making real progress toward your goals.

Facing challenges and discomfort head-on will also help you grow emotionally. Every obstacle you overcome strengthens your resilience and builds your confidence.

With each step forward, you'll notice a growing sense of empowerment as you realize you're no longer reacting to life but actively shaping it.

Taking responsibility for your actions and responses creates puts you in control and gives you self-assurance.

You'll discover that you have the ability to navigate life's events with purpose and intention, transforming setbacks into stepping stones. This mindset shift leads to meaningful progress and fulfillment, as every decision aligns with your bigger vision.

By embracing ownership of your future, you'll create space to celebrate your growth and achievements.

Congratulations!

Each action you take will bring you closer to the life you truly want, filling you with a deep sense of satisfaction and pride.

You're not just chasing change—you're creating a life that feels purposeful, rewarding, and truly your own.

TAKE ACTION TODAY: CREATE YOUR BEST LIFE

You've gained valuable tools and strategies throughout this book, and now it's time to put them into action.

Reading and learning are powerful first steps, but the real magic happens when you apply what you've discovered to your own life.

Reflect on the areas where you want to grow—whether it's improving decision-making, focusing on meaningful results, embracing challenges, or taking ownership of your responses.

Then, **choose one meaningful step you can take today to move forward.**

It could be revisiting a decision with a long-term perspective, addressing a challenge you've been avoiding, or shifting your mindset to focus on solutions.

Whatever it is, commit to that action now.

This isn't about perfection—it's about progress.

Every action you take brings you closer to the thriving life you truly want. You've got everything you need to succeed, so let's start building the future you want!

FINAL THOUGHTS

If there's one thing to carry with you from this book, let it be this: **You have more power than you may realize.**

Life is full of opportunities, and while challenges will arise, you have the mindset, strength, and resilience to navigate them with confidence and purpose.

You hold the ability to shape a life filled with meaning, growth, and joy—one choice, one decision, one empowering action at a time.

Each step forward brings you closer to the future you envision.

So, here's to your incredible journey.

Here's to embracing your potential, making choices that align with your dreams, and living with the freedom that comes from taking ownership of your life.

You've got everything you need to thrive.

Your future is waiting—go out and create something extraordinary!

Congratulations!

THE EIGHT KEYS

The Master Key: Get Started. Keep Going

1 **Future-Proof Your Decisions** – The choices you make today create your future—this key helps you think beyond quick wins and make decisions that set you up for lasting success.

2 **Work Smart to Finish Strong** – Being busy isn't the same as being effective—this key helps you focus on what truly moves you ahead and follow through so your hard work creates real impact.

3 **Ask Better Questions and Thrive Faster** – The questions you ask shape the opportunities you see—start asking better questions, and you'll unlock new possibilities, deeper understanding, and smarter decisions.

4 **Find the Sweet Spot Between Passion, Strengths & Practicality** – Thriving isn't just about chasing passion—it's about balancing what you love, what matters, and what actually works in the real world.

5 **Dream Boldly and See Clearly** – Big dreams drive success, but real progress comes from balancing ambition with a clear understanding of reality—so you can take practical steps toward making your vision happen.

6 **Use Identity Instead of Willpower** – The fastest way to lasting change is shifting how you see yourself—because when your actions align with your identity, success becomes second nature.

7 **Transform Pain Into Power** – Pain isn't something to avoid—it's a signal guiding you toward growth, strength, and resilience when you learn to listen and transform it into progress.

8 **Turn Challenge into Choice** – You can't control everything that happens, but you can control how you respond—this key helps you turn obstacles into opportunities by owning your reactions.

www.ingramcontent.com/pod-product-compliance
Lightning Source LLC
Chambersburg PA
CBHW060823050426
42453CB00008B/560